THESE ENVOYS OF BEAUTY

Anna Vaught is an English teacher, mentor and author of several books, including 2020's novel *Saving Lucia* and short fiction collection, *Famished*. Her shorter and multi-genre works are widely published in journals, magazines and anthologies. She is currently a columnist for *Mslexia* and has written regularly for *The Bookseller*, including as a columnist. Anna's second short fiction collection, *Ravished*, was published by Reflex Press in 2022, and 2023 will see five books: memoir, *These Envoys of Beauty* (Reflex Press), new novel *The Zebra and Lord Jones*, plus *The Alchemy*, Anna's first book about writing (both Renard Press, UK and Commonwealth). *Saving Lucia* will be published in Italian by Milan's 8tto Edizioni as *Bang Bang Mussolini*. Anna is a guest university lecturer, tutor for Jericho Writers, volunteer with young people, creator of the new Curae prize for writer-carers, with industry-wide support, and the editor of *Curae: An Anthology from the Inaugural Prize* (Renard Press, 2023). She works alongside chronic illness, is a passionate campaigner for mental health provision, including in the publishing industry, and she is represented by Kate Johnson of Wolf Literary, NYC. Anna has just finished a collection of essays and is working on a new novel and second memoir.

These Envoys of Beauty

Anna Vaught

REFLEX PRESS

First published in 2023 by Reflex Press
Abingdon, Oxfordshire, OX14 3SY
www.reflex.press

A CIP catalogue record of this book is
available from the British Library.

ISBN: 978-1-914114-11-3

1 3 5 7 9 10 8 6 4 2

Printed and bound in Great Britain by
Severn.

Cover image by New Africa

www.reflex.press/these-envoys-of-beauty/

This book is dedicated to my darling sons
Love you forever.
Mum
x

Please be aware that this book is about personal experience and includes accounts of or references to mental ill health, OCD, self-harming, suicide, depression, anxiety, dissociation, and derealisation. Also, to violence and cruelty within a family. Importantly, some of these experiences were lived through by a child so please read mindfully.

To go into solitude, a man needs to retire as much from his chamber as from society. I am not solitary whilst I read and write, though nobody is with me. But if a man would be alone, let him look at the stars. The rays that come from those heavenly worlds, will separate between him and what he touches. One might think the atmosphere was made transparent with this design, to give man, in the heavenly bodies, the perpetual presence of the sublime. Seen in the streets of cities, how great they are! If the stars should appear one night in a thousand years, how would men believe and adore; and preserve for many generations the remembrance of the city of God which had been shown! But every night come out these envoys of beauty and light the universe with their admonishing smile.

Ralph Waldo Emerson. From 'Nature', Chapter One.[1]

---

1. Ralph Waldo Emerson, *Selected Essays, Lectures and Poems*, ed. Robert D. Richardson, Bantam 1990, 2007. 'Nature' was written in 1836.

A NOTE ON THE TEXT

All epigraphs are from Ralph Waldo Emerson's 1836 essay 'Nature', as is the title of the book (shown in the first longer epigraph), I have included botanical names for all plants and trees because they are so beautiful and I thought readers might enjoy seeing them, too. As a kid, I loved to learn them and would roll the names around in my mouth. Like sweeties. Only Latin is better for you in the mouth than butterscotch. The photographs included are all recent ones of my own.

CONTENTS

(Early morning roses in our wild garden.)

Introduction

So shall we come to look at the world with new eyes.

There are twelve essays in *These Envoys of Beauty*, and each looks at some element – or elements – in the natural world and what they have meant to me. When I say that, I mean how I look at it, how I feel, how that has changed, but, for the scope of this book, what any of it has to do with trauma and its management. Let me explain.

I grew up very rurally, raised by a Welsh family on the Somerset-Wiltshire border, but I have habitually spent a great deal of time in West Wales, particularly Pembrokeshire, because that is where most of my family is from. I now live in West Wiltshire. Open land, woods, riverbanks were and are my world. I am also sure that they are how I survived – not better, but more or less intact.

What I show you in this book rests on formative incidents as a child and adolescent: bookish, nerdy, and socially awkward (all of which I still am, only I do not mind now). I spent as much time outside as possible and was always scrambling about somewhere, up trees, in ditches, into rivers and streams and home to look things up and, sometimes, preserve specimens in books or a flower press – or found antique treasures in pillboxes and tins. That is still me today. If you had looked in my primary school books or those in the early years of secondary school, what I wanted to be when I grew up was a botanist. I would spend hours out there and, afterwards, hours in there, looking at my guides and drawing plants and animals – a particularly tame wren on the dog roses, a tree mallow with its flowers open to the sun, looking happy. *Lavatera arborea*: I loved the rhythm of those words as a child and would linger there now.

I was raised on the crest of a hill, with orchards and old woods behind me and the fields below me and to one side, the river Frome in the valley, near to where it meets the Avon. The Wiltshire sign was below our house but parallel with a lower wall, and I was always delighted that where I lived straddled two counties. I must have thought this was unique back then. Or forbidden: you had to live in one place or another, not in two. Then, the time in Wales: St Brides Bay, Cardigan Bay, the islands – Ramsey, Skomer and Skokholm – and the water lands; the Daugleddau estuary where my grandmother had once lived, where part of it ended at Cresswell Quay. There were other places that felt like a home, too – Cardiff Bay, the Brecon Beacons and the Black Mountains – and I have always felt more Welsh than English because I was raised by Welsh people in England. I feel that within me, and I like the way the two things tangle, itself a story for another book.

I was so lucky in many ways, and I am very aware of the privilege of growing up in these places. This is one story: bluebells, wild garlic, wood aconites, red campion, mud and flood and feeling the lichen and moss and stone stiles.

But there is a second story.

I did not understand the dynamics of my immediate family; that I was blessed in where I lived made me think it was terrible to confess it, and I am not sure who I could tell. There was deep weirdness, death, unspoken illness and psychiatric problems the nature of which I did not understand in my father's family, and, since the day he died, when I was eighteen, I have not seen them: they cut me off, just like that, my world there and everything that it brought into my imagination at first, had disappeared. I did not understand at first that its best bits could live on in that imagination, lively and fresh, though wrought by that deep weirdness. Then, my parents and sibling. I did not understand and still do not, and because I have explored it elsewhere and it is not the main thrust of the book – though you can see and infer much, reading through – I will not do so. But there were events which still, as I write, make me feel unsettled. My mouth becomes dry, and I am under threat. I do not expect to get better from this. It is all because of my mother. She was a splendid woman, and I loved her, really, against my will. Because although there were streaks of that splendidness with me, what I was given and what I was left with was the sense that I was evil, the bringer of harm, a blot, a brat, a harlot, a slut, a terrible, selfish thing. This, she would always tell me, even when I was small, was what everyone else thought too. I did not know any different.

She would slap me, pull my hair, kick me when I had fallen and scratch at my ears, but mostly it was the words. The confusion lay, as I say, because I grew up in a beautiful place. I could see that, empirically, but I knew it, hard, because my parents had come from large working-class rural families and had made the ascent, they would say, to the middle classes or were very much on the way. It makes sense that they should want to remind me of blessings. But, you see, my mother also repeatedly told me I did not deserve it. She was ill a great deal, and I remember feeling sick and shivering at the tension in the house. She took the time to tell me that I had made her worse. Then, when I was thirteen, my father became ill. The descent was slow at first, then rapid and dizzying. I did my best to help them both, to care for them, while feeling that I was a burden and blot and then came the day that I was told I had hastened his death. I had always worried I was capable of this. Now it had come true.

At night, I would recite Latin names from plant books like mantras and talismans. I had awful ruminating and intrusive thoughts. I would feel a bad thought about someone ushering in – not something I actually felt, but a collocation of words in my head; a fit of diction, that was all. But by the time I was seven or eight, it was so entrenched that I was a bringer of harm that I decided I had to expel the words so as not to make the dreadful thing happen. I would have to go and tell that person, always an adult, a dinner lady, a teacher, the school caretaker, the vicar. What they thought I cannot imagine, but I do not remember reassurance ever being given.

By my late teens, I had developed severe anxiety, depression. I first tried to take my own life when I was fifteen and again when I was nineteen. On the first of those occasions, my mother would not take me to hospital but instead said I should go to my room. I did not tell anyone this until after the birth of my first child, when I was dreadfully unwell and being looked after by a consultant psychiatrist in outpatients and a kindly GP. This is the first time I have written about it. I don't know whether she hoped I would die – I had taken a considerable amount of paracetamol – or if it was simply too much for her to think about. I did not understand then, and I still don't and will never have the opportunity to ask. Both my parents were dead by the time I became an adult.

From the age of twenty-one, I have been in and out of care – such as is available – and, ever since my teens, I have had difficult periods of varying length and intensity, where I don't know where or quite who I am; where my edges are. It is exhausting. My parents never talked about it and did not try to help me. My mother said mental health problems were an indulgence. She said moods were a myth, especially moods in teenagers, a licence for bad behaviour. PMT, she said, was made up. People who were mentally ill were those who had failed to control themselves. I don't know why she said these things, but I feel now, looking back, that there was such burning life in her which had been thwarted. Moreover, mental illness – and severe mental illness – was rife on both sides of my family, and I wonder if neither of my parents could bear to accept it within our family home. They rejected it because they were frightened and wanted to retain control and function; in doing so, they created something that was dysfunctional. Any one of us can be ill – and any one of us can have things go wrong with our mind.

I remember that it often felt so cold in our house, though a fire was often lit. I remember the day when my mother bought lamps as a development from the days of big light. I felt like we had arrived, and I loved the soft pools of light which fell on the floor and then, wonders, beside my bed. But you see, that softness did not last, and it was cosmetic. I looked outside.

Oh, there was a lot more than I feel I can tell which went on, but you can infer as we go because the point of this book is not degradation and terror but joy and survival. Of course, I learned a good deal from some – not all! – of my therapy received sporadically over the decades of adulthood, but all that

19

time, today, this afternoon, it was my connection with the natural world (and my reading)[2] and all things in it which shored me up. On my worst days, I cannot go far, so I am just outside and listening intently. I am a rural girl, but I am observing wherever I go.

In this book, stay with me as I show you the world I explored and what it meant to me then and now. The essays are not chronological but dart back and forth between them and within, memories and ideas associating and cohering. I do not mean to mythologise nature because it is also full of facts, and yet it illuminates, calms, and makes things intelligible. Sometimes I feel it as a metaphor, sometimes just as a sense or a reminder or prod – in the hard lines of something or the delicate feather of rime – to think about something with a different attitude. Also, even when it is small about me, I perceive space; that is how it was for me as a child.

I constantly refer back to the natural world to try and discover who I am, remember what I was, or even think about how I could be. In his book *Nature Cure*, Richard Mabey notes, in writing about depression, that he believed the natural world was the most powerful source of metaphors to describe and explain behaviour and feelings,[3] which is true, I think. When I was very young, and would run out or just stand and stare, I would look to plants and trees to help me explain to myself a bewildering world. There was something else, encapsulated by Wilson A. Bentley, known as 'The Snowflake Man,'

---

2. If you like, you can read an account of reading, the imagination and survival in an essay I wrote for *Trauma: An Anthology of Writing about Art and Mental Health*, Dodo Ink, ed Mills and Cuell, 2021. It also uses some sections from my first book, which was a work of autobiographical fiction.

3. *Nature Cure*, Richard Mabey, Chatto & Windus, 2005, Little Toller, 2021, p. 32 gives a wonderfully precise description of this.

who studied the snow and published many extraordinary photomicrographs of snowflakes. Bentley saw the snowflakes, as he observed them from Jericho, in Vermont, as a metaphor for all things beautiful on earth, but he also thought they were a reminder of how earthly beauty was transient and would fade. That did not stop his joy and curiosity in studying them so closely. In the ephemeral nature of phenomena, however, he also found comfort, because while the beauty of the snow was evanescent, like the seasons, or the stars he saw in the evening sky, it would fade but always come again. Being a quiet observer, a student of nature, is such a salve.[4]

I want to reiterate. Nature has not been my cure. It has been my inspiration, teacher, and companion. I am not better, but I have never been alone.

---

4. There are many lovely observations of this kind in *The Snowflake Man: A Biography of Wilson A. Bentley*, Duncan Blanchard, Macdonald and Woodward Publishing Company, 1998.

(Shells: North Beach, Tenby, Pembrokeshire.)

Rosebay willowherb and a cure for loneliness

Nature is a setting that fits equally well a comic or a
mourning piece.

Rosebay – my willowherb of choice: *Chamaenerion angusti-*
folium – with its full and fuchsia family. Have you ever looked
at the plant and spent time with it, observing it as it bursts
open and delicate filigree webbing holds seeds that blow out
into the world? Cotton and gossamer; magic. Varieties are
everywhere, and I venerate them: by the side of the M4 mo-
torway, by the least promising layby on the A55, and in the
past on a rough and tumble bank in Somerset, where I grew
up. I knew, even as a small child, from my *Collins Complete*
Guide to British Wildlife.[5] That willowherb had a rough and
tumble family, too. There is the New Zealand willowherb, a
latter-day interloper, marsh, great, broad leaf (the most common), and square-stemmed. In my experience, a lot of people
do not seem to know what they are called, though they recog-
nise them, seeing them only as weeds or a sort of pretender

5. *Collins Complete Guide to British Wildlife*, Richard and Alistair Fitter,
1981.

to foxglove. The rosebay was always my favourite because of its lovely name, and the play of syllables seemed particularly pretty, and because on the rough and tumble bank, it was abundant, and I loved the filigree and cotton and would come in covered with the stuff, racing to get it off my clothes. I would hide amongst those stiffly erect stems and unequal petals, and how fine the name in Latin is: say it aloud, trippingly on your tongue: *Epilobium angustifolium*. My maternal grandmother called it fireweed, and my father said you could not kill it – which was exactly what I liked about it. It thrived.

The fireweed description stuck because I thought of it as both beautiful and angry, resilient, in a way I was not yet but hoped to be. It revelled in its untidy smudges on the rough and tumble bank, and I knew it would come back repeatedly; I knew I would see it thrive everywhere I looked. There is a piercing memory erupting each time I think of it: this is about another bank, a long one underneath a laundry line on the edge of an orchard, and there I went on my third birthday. I have always been told that I could not possibly remember this birthday, but I can feel and see it vividly, and I know I was wearing pink and looking at yellow and together, pink and yellow, we were the colour of rhubarb and custard sweets. The faces of the celandines (*Ficaria verna*, the lesser celandine but also some greater celandines, *Chelidonium majus*)[6] and

6. The greater celandine is also known as swallow-wort because it's said to start flowering – I have never seen evidence for this! – when the swallows arrive in the British Isles, the origin of its name also derives, ultimately, from the Greek for swallow: it's a member of the poppy family. The lesser celandine is actually not related to the greater as it is a member of the buttercup family; Wordsworth was fond of it: 'There's a flower that shall be mine, 'Tis the little Celandine.' William Wordsworth, 'To the Small Celandine'. There are two other poems to the flower. The lesser celandine traditionally first blooms on the 21st of February, making it one of the first woodland flowers of the year. This

opened to the sun. That small girl was standing on a soft bank in a spring breeze as the laundry blew high above her there in the orchard. The breeze blew cold, but there were currents of warmth about her legs as the day decided whether it would whip or kiss. Sitting now, legs akimbo on the bank, that little girl who was me saw the faces of the yellow celandines open to the sun, the hedge full of primroses beyond the whirling laundry, and she was happy. Just as she was bathed in hope and fire by the rosebay willowherb, here was more bathing: she knew that she could bury her face in the violet patch and lounge there with their sweetness. That is, for a short while, because this child always knew that after such delicacy came danger and threat, and there was no one to tell. But if you know that the faces of the celandines open to the sun, time and again, and the willowherb rebels however much you tidy and cut, there is an angry power to that, felt even by a small child.

This plant comforts me now, as it did through my child-hood and teenage years. You could be near it almost anywhere, which was a comfort to me, and it always came back if you mowed it, scythed it or tried to destroy and sterilise the ground around it: it was always a sign, for me, not of a weed, a not important plant, but of something blessedly important, fa-miliar, immortal and a haven for bees – there are few things I like more than bees. If, as a child, you are surrounded by a sort of passionate morbidity, by a frightening psychiatric incident

also gave the lesser celandine the name 'spring messenger'. Researching Victorian botanicals shows you that, being seen as a herald of spring, it used to symbolise 'joys to come'. One of its regional names is 'pilewort' since the herb was given for haemorrhoids. This was based on the doc-trine of signatures since the knobbly tubers were thought to resemble piles. I knew it by this name in Somerset and South Wales, although my maternal grandmother and extended family referred to it as a buttercup.

in the family – which is frightening because it is spoken of behind closed doors and with euphemism – it may be that you need to latch on to things around you which provide stability and reassurance. Much of this was in the natural world for me, often accompanied by a book: in fire, fuchsia and the flagrancy of thrown seed and cotton threads.

On drinking from leaves and bells. Creating hope

Nature never wears a mean appearance.

There is a scramble over an unstable wall, past den-creepers and nettle beds, along animal trails. Then, down a muddy bank, cross a little road with a sharp bend where there is a county boundary – Wiltshire into Somerset – and into the cowslip field.

You need to lie beside the cowslips, *Primula veris*, on a warm day because then their spicy scent is particularly delicious, and the velvet of the bell is so soft under your hand because it was kissed by the sun.

I could not and cannot always interpret why some fields spoke to me – why I never tried to enter this place at any other time of year, or if I should. But let us try. Do you know? Is it memory? Something spiritual or perhaps an indefinable presence which says, 'Don't come in; this place is not for you?' Or are you not seeing it correctly? It is a field rich in life and details: how could it harm or fail to welcome you? Perhaps the answer is that your view of the world is only, as the late Australian psychologist Dorothy Rowe described it, a series of pictures; that is, one only sees the world the way one has learned to see it. People see depth and distance differently; they perceive shapes and movement, expression, colour, a tree, a smile, emotional tenor and all the things in the world in varying ways. They do not even notice others because what we see as important and what we overlook depends on past experience. In other words, our picture of the world is something we have created.'[7]

So here is and was the challenge: to see clearly and thus to parse what you think is a series of unwelcoming signs; to look at banks, the cups of flowers – like gorse, *Ulex europaeus*, and ask, is that place or are those things for me? May I come in? And, in my case, *would they help me*?

Let me tell you about something I hoped would be a fine time, and in the most roundabout way, we will get to cups and bells. This is focused on my father, a figure I struggle to see or find an outline of. He died when I was eighteen but had withdrawn from me some years before, and had beena private, unknowable man in the years before. It is so odd. All these shadowy forms. But let us try to give him and a particular memory a little substance.

As a child and young person, I was often aware of a tension in my body, as if it were not calibrated properly. I remember having a lot of stomach aches and tight bands around my head but assumed this was how everyone felt. but learned it was not the case, as you shall see. There were times, however, in floods, standing on a wobbly and moss-covered wall by a

_____

7. Dorothy Rowe, *Depression. The Way Out Of Your Prison*, Routledge 2003, Chapter 3, page 15 summarises this beautifully; when I first read her description of how we construct meaning, it seemed both revolutionary and blindingly obvious. Because the natural extension of thinking about how we construct meaning is that, if we address the how, we can deconstruct what we made, if it does not serve us.

country lane, jumping over an old stone stile or pelting into the sea when the symptoms abated. Even now, if I am out of sorts or fearful, I like to run on a beach and, still, helter-skelter into the sea. There was one particular time, a fine time I had hoped, when freedom beckoned and the dull sense of problems coiling and uncoiling would begin to abate, and this was a project for me and my father to walk, in stretches, the whole of the Pembrokeshire Coast Path. To this day, I think that this is the finest coastline I have seen, though it holds such piercing memories of St Bride's Bay on a fine day and setting out to understand said father: really, it was *his* project; I just happened to be there, but it would beat bad-tempered crochet with my mother in the family caravan. And she *hated* that caravan. Up and down, climbing over the rocks, occasionally, or at least this is how I remember it, perilously close to the cliff edge or along thickets of gnarled, lichen-covered trees, we did a different stage each day. I climbed on rocks at the water's edge, took the force of the wave in my face, coming up new for a while and chewing on bladderwrack – *Fucus vesiculosus, Fucus vesiculosus, Fucus vesiculosus*; I used to repeat those words and lie about in their sibilance[8] – seaweed. The cormorants eyed me suspiciously, sleek and stretching out their wet wings to sun and breeze. Out there in the bay, I could see – I show my youngest son now; only this summer we went tanker spotting – the great tankers waiting to come into Pembroke Dock or Milford Haven, or perhaps they were setting out for balmy climes. To *where*? Somewhere tropical, perhaps? Out there, to the heart of darkness and down a deep,

---

8. I have always loved its other names, too: the ones I know are bladderwrack, black tang, rockweed, sea grapes, bladder fucus, sea oak, cut weed, dyers fucus, red fucus and rock wrack, but it may be that there are other names.

wide river that was an inscrutable force of nature, old as time. Looking far out to sea, it always felt to me that the tankers carried a tinge of the supernatural with them; they might have been cresting warm waves weeks ago, visited by flying fish and graced with cinnamon and warm spices: these were soft nuances they carried into colder waters.

When I was small (now I was a teenager because we walked this path again and again until he was too ill and was going slightly mad and wanted to spend time there on his own, quiet, and preparing to die) I imagined myself like a pretty little mermaid on the rock: 'But sailors, sailors: *take me with you. Take me away from this.* I will grow up on your boats and cook for you and not break anything, and when I am old enough and big enough, maybe you will fall in love with me with my long shining hair!

The coast walks were, apart from visits to grandad and jobs in the garden, the only time I spent with my father. To me, he was then, as he is now, incomplete; shadowy; an unknowable figure. I could have told you everything about his accomplishments and his hobbies and about how hard he worked, though: so that had to be *knowing* enough. He was a silent man (apart from the episodes of badger cursing and shouting at anything, human or feral, which got near the prized caravan, which, as I said, my mother hated), but a teacher; wood smith and wordsmith; creator of fires; fine cricketer; lay preacher: many lives in one. He had survived the dour peculiarities of his own family home, was mad for petrol lawnmowers with their craft and their finely calibrated maintenance, chainsaws, and the correct manner of cleaving logs (done with mathematical precision). Yet he was intensely accident-prone. He had cut off a big toe in a lawn mower accident and twice severed his thumb in the workshop – once as I watched. On an otherwise quiet but thumb-severing Sunday, my face was hit by the ricochet of blood; one other Sunday, as the light dimmed, he felled a tree and ran the wrong way, so the tree felled him. I pulled him out. But he was angry with me, I had thought: not himself or even a particularly wilful tree. (Here I should gloss that I did not understand why my parents were so often extremely angry with me. It was something I must frequently have been doing, but I did not comprehend its nature.)

An apocryphal tale – and there were many apocryphal tales involving blood loss or ruptured arteries – about my paternal family had it that during military service, he had fallen asleep, standing up, under the inspection hatch of a plane; it fell open against his head, and he lost most of his teeth; in my young imagination and partly because my paternal grandfather always told the most blood-curdling stories of mangling and squishing and uncles dying between the buffers of trains or the horse that suddenly turned, my father had accrued a sense of danger and threat around him. You can hardly say it was his fault. I remember the tooth plates which stood, at night, weirdly yellow and magenta candy-coloured as they fizzed in glasses in the bathroom. But who he was, I did not really know, although I had felt his blood on my skin. So, in my teenage years, as we walked, I would try to talk to him about thrift, seabirds, or whether the cormorants that had scrutinised me on the rocks could be trained to dive down and fish and come back up and drop their catch, as I had read they were in China or Southern India. And once, particularly daring but really against my better judgement, I asked him *A Difficult Question*. I said, knowing that my parents spoke so highly of Number One Son[9] – of how easy and gentle he was,

9. I am not an only child, but that I am not is only alluded to in the book so our focus on the natural world is not entirely lost.

while I stayed an eldritch child, 'Dad, can I ask you something? I want... for you to tell me something?'

'Oh! What is it *now*?' The watery grey-granite eyes looked past me, and I recall that I looked past *them*, early teen awkwardness in full throttle, touching the gorse and looking at a crumbling edge of the coast path and wondering what they were doing on that tanker, out there in the Irish sea.

'I think I want some reassurance. I mean, I'm sorry, I mean that I know Mum doesn't like me and that I am a trial and all, but—'

'For Christ's sake, get on with it. I want to identify that bird on the rock there and can't if you keep talking.'

He was going to say it was a cormorant, but I knew it was a shag.[10] Shags are birds of the coast. Occasionally, they turn up inland along rivers and lakes, but usually alone (cormorants are often seen in groups inland). The shag's beak is more delicate than the cormorant's, and the forehead angle is steeper. These were my thoughts, rattling through my head as is quite common for children and young people who are seabird nerds. But if my father had said it was a cormorant, I would have agreed.

'Well, when you talk about me, do you say that I'm, that I'm, well, okay?' His answer was blunt. 'We prefer to spend

10. Cormorants and shags belong to the group *Phalacrocoracidae*, which is a family of about forty species of aquatic birds commonly known as cormorants and shags. When wearing their breeding plumage, they are quite easy to tell apart because the cormorant has a white thigh patch, while the shag has a recurved short wispy crest and dark thighs. At other times of the year, it is the difference in size and shape that you look for: cormorants have a bigger, more triangular head, a flatter forehead and a more massive bill, giving an angular, almost wedge-shaped look to the head, while shags are significantly smaller, shorter and more slender. I have always been a seaside nerd. It rescued me many times, too.

time with our Number One Son. He listens to us; he likes to be with us, and he never says a word. And you should know you are here *under sufferance*. Now pass me the bird spotter.'

'But I listen. It is how I know you like cormorants (I did not mention the shag, alone on the rocks below) and thrift and caravans.' And now there was silence. The warmth of the banks pulsed about me; I remember that so clearly. I looked at the gorse, bright yellow, and stroked it, then pricked my fingers on it to frighten my senses into something better; that is, a more understandable, more rational sort of fear. I have always remembered this conversation. Sometimes, if I sit quietly, up it comes, and it is the coldness of the eyes on a warm day that I remember most. It makes no sense to me when I remember the advice I overheard him giving to parents: 'Never crush a child's spirit' being an important phrase. But the sufferance, the plainly preferred sibling, the palpable disappointment in and plain dislike of the daughter; it rankled on the clearest day: 'He never says a word. You are talking.' I could not keep quiet because the words were so beautiful, whatever risks they brought with them. I am not sure I can now. I will tell you something else. The thing that salvaged that day when, by impulse, I might have hurled myself off the cliff. It was the gorse: I touched it again, feeling the velvet pods and sachets of the flower and the prickle of the stems.

Then I plucked a gorse flower and sucked hard on it.

You could try it too: it tastes of coconut, working best if you close your eyes. I do not know who taught me to do this or whether it was just trial and error because I was always pinching shoots, putting things in my mouth, making my fingers bleed. Associating wildly.

I will be honest with you, reader. I feel queasy writing this, and my heart drops like a stone. I feel sweaty, and a shiver spreads across my shoulders and sweeps round across my collarbones. It is as if the situation is in the room, around me; judgement and clarity on this nasty little drone as broad as day, spreading out into the world so everyone can see who and what I am. I have never changed, and it is just like they said.[11]

And I do not know if I decided this then, but I had clarified that, in a situation which was so wildly confusing, I would fall back on my senses in the simplest way. Here, a drag on the tiny pocket of coconut-flavour nectar at the base of the gorse flower: xanthic, royal and lemon – those were its shade of yellow. Here: think that the world is only the series of pictures which you made, pictures which were often prompted by others, your elders, and betters, who told you some things were incontrovertibly true. It is the work of the imagination to tease that apart and think, what do I see? What do I feel? Will it let me in? Yes, it will: you may drink from its cups and bells on a day when you are at sea.

It is not for other people: *it is for you*. Drink.

And another thing about the gorse flower: picture its strident and assertive yellow against a watery colour. A colour that does not seem to wish you well, but you do not know why and cannot ask. I *think* I loved my father – and my mother, so

---

11. There is a helpful description of what this is in many places, but I have chosen Mind, the British mental health charity, for an explanation. Essentially, because of things which happened to me, I have vivid flashbacks (feeling like the trauma is happening right now), intrusive thoughts or images, recurrent nightmares, intense distress at real or symbolic reminders of things I found traumatic and physical sensations such as pain, sweating, nausea or trembling.
https://www.mind.org.uk/information-support/types-of-mental-health-problems/post-traumatic-stress-disorder-ptsd-and-complex-ptsd/symptoms/ and https://www.mind.org.uk/information-support/types-of-mental-health-problems/post-traumatic-stress-disorder-ptsd-and-complex-ptsd/complex-ptsd/

pretty with her similarly watery blue eyes – but then I suppose it is more the idea of them because so much went terribly wrong and because I did not know either of them as an adult, or my sibling. When panic rises, and I see the watery blue, I close my eyes and raise beside it that strident yellow and feel better.

When something pops up in your mind's eye, so strong, that wishes *you were not*, that tells you *you cannot be loved, ought not to be in the world, are not deserving of any good things*, promise me this: replace it with something stronger: my yellow punch for the cold, limp touch of your dimming sapphire. Or your blazing fire for a sad, damp fireplace that warms and beckons no one.

(Descent from the headland to Barafundle, Pembrokeshire.)

On depression: flood and mud

To speak truly, few adult persons can see nature.
Most persons do not see the sun. At least they have a
very superficial seeing. The sun illuminates only the
eye of the man, but shines into the eye and the heart
of the child.

To have depression is, in my experience, to experience things through a glass darkly. To feel isolated in a crowd. In a playground as a child or later, when more grown, walking down a busy street, it is as if there is a sheet of glass between you and others; a troubling disconnect between you and the people around you, so that kind words cannot penetrate. It took me a long time to realise that I must have had periods of depression throughout my childhood because of the way I would look at things without really feeling them. I often felt separate and odd, and yet, I still knew there was this pulsing sense of life within me.

It was the natural world which allowed me to see clearly, as best I can describe it. When I first started writing about my experiences in the early 2000s as explanatory notes to offer to therapists – because I became terribly ill after the birth of my first child – I wrote above movements, depths and tides. I meant them literally, as a place of love and solace, but also as metaphor: that what I saw and lived in I also tried to link to my mind and the way I could make it work: layers and stretches of water that others could not cross. Does that make any sense at all?

I loved the rivers and the places where they spilled into fields so you could not quite see what was edge and what was water. I loved soils and mud, and when I was particularly upset, I would go out and try to pull up clay from the soil nearby and mould it into tiny pots which collapsed straight away, but even so, they had existed, and I had dug them out. I loved the smell of that heavy clay soil, its feel, and I would taste it just as I would lick bark and drink from leaves.

I grew up in a beautiful place, but a sense of safety and comfortable enclosure were best achieved through the pages of a book, so I invariably turned to 'The Wild Wood' chapter in *The Wind in the Willows* (knowing that Mole would escape its dangers in a hollow and with the aid of Ratty with a stout cudgel), the home of Mr Badger and the snowy journey through the fields in 'Dulce Domum'. But there is a chapter I am coming to that would make me cry and feel helpless and lonely as a child, yet I wanted to read it repeatedly. Once, after lingering on stories from *The Wind in the Willows*, I canvassed my primary school classmates on their opinions of the book and thus it was that a peculiarity arose: none of them remembered a particular chapter – and this caused her to wonder whether it had been imagined in a dream by day or night: 'The Piper at the Gates of Dawn'. It wasn't the notion of the child otter having wandered off, held safe by the great creature, the friend and helper, and found again by his father, but rather that it is about mystery: of something deeply felt but faintly, inchoately understood. On hearing the pipes of Pan, Ratty knows he has found the *place of my song dream*, and when the moment is passed, Mole stands still for a moment, held in thought. It is as if he has been suddenly woken from a beautiful dream he struggles to recall; the poor creature can recapture nothing but a dim sense of the beauty of it all, and that beauty fades away in turn, and Mole, the dreamer, bitterly accepts the hard cold waking to the world, with all its penalties. To me, it was like Caliban, who 'cried to dream again'. I sat, as a young teenager, without a world of interest in the play, until I heard these lines and a delineation of what I wanted, in a dream, a different place, a kind lacuna between the world of sleep and the other world.

> *Be not afeard. The isle is full of noises,*
> *Sounds, and sweet airs, that give delight, and hurt not.*
> *Sometimes a thousand twangling instruments*
> *Will hum about mine ears, and sometime voices,*
> *That if I then had waked after long sleep*
> *Will make me sleep again; and then in dreaming*
> *The clouds methought would open and show riches*
> *Ready to drop upon me, that when I waked*
> *I cried to dream again.*[12]

Oh, I certainly understood *cold waking* – I had many nights of that, frightened, alone and convinced of appalling sin, wetting the bed in her fear. *Penalties* were part of life, sporadically most of my life, and definitely the consequence of happiness, as I had instinctively known one perfect day in the orchard,

---

12. William Shakespeare's *The Tempest*, Act III, scene II.

caressed momentarily by deferential celandines and the warm threads of breeze. It was my third birthday. I would yearn to find this place and its feeling of sadness, but also of inscrutability and throbbing, growing faith. And so, into the nearby landscape, I would run, early and before anyone noticed, to the fields and the weir. I was looking for something only I could see. Running out early was not allowed, but it was worth the gamble. Yet would I ever find the kindness of a great creature there? Of a great *thing*? Hope almost exhausted, I would lie down in the wet grass and weep there, knowing that the land retained a memory, sweet, sad, and buried, of something extraordinary there in the sods, by the pounding of the water. One day. *One* day.

A place of no penalties.

There is one incident that makes me shudder – I want to say now that I am a mother myself, but I think anyone can understand just by imagining the small child who said it. On Christmas Day, and I think it was my seventh, possibly eighth Christmas, I seemed to have more presents than usual because a few friends of the family had also given me some money, and an aunt had been particularly generous. My mother scowled at me. Her face said, *This is so much more than you deserve*, and I remember that my delight turned sour, and I felt a shiver of fear – reader, I can feel it now as I write these words, and I can see the hostility in my mother's eyes – and so I said, aloud, 'I could go to my room?' She said nothing, so I tried to give her the money. Two five-pound notes. She flipped them away. So, I said, 'You can hit me if you like,' and she kept looking at me, said nothing, and then went into the kitchen and closed the door. The life of contrarieties: that shivering child, and we will have had a lovely Christmas dinner. Just like the beautiful birthday cakes, it caused me such confusion because how could I be cared for in this way and still be told I was not wanted, that I was an eldritch child?

Nature offered stability and satisfying detail; pattern, form and things that made sense.

Feeling mud in my hands was another way to connect and soothe, and that way I had to try to make the momentary clay pots. Also, observing the strata, the distinct levels and colour of the mud as you plunged your wellies into it, in the fields during rainy November. Or the floods that seemed to come near Christmas and, particularly, around my birthday in mid-February. I would walk in the fields, slightly too close to the river's edge, blurred, as I told you. Then, I would sit and skim stones from the little mud islands on the edge of the river Frome, where the water was most shallow, or I would wade out, sometimes out of my depth or nearly so, and feel the roots protruding from the banks and bend so that the water weeds seeped between my fingers and slapped the back of my hands. If there was a river or a stream, I had to get in it, and that has never, ever changed. Along with the urge to put my hands in, feel the bank, the stones, to build a small dam and sometimes disassemble it just to watch what happens.

Again, depression is, in my experience, to experience things through a glass darkly. To feel isolated in a crowd. In a playground as a child or later, when more grown, walking down a busy street, it is as if there is a sheet of glass between you and others; a troubling disconnect between you and the people around you, so that kind words cannot penetrate.

But water, weeds and mud do not judge; they just *are*. Put them on your hands, and I challenge you to build a dam very soon, though I am compelled to ask you to be in a moderate stream, at most. If not, touch the soil because it is always there, nearby, and have a glass of water. I think about Philip

Larkin's poem 'Water' sometimes – particularly the first verse; the centrality of this object, substance: how soothing, salving and varied it is in all its incarnations. Look at it: *really look at it, still or moving.* To me, this remains one of the greatest comforts. So, when Philip Larkin stated that if he were called to construct a religion, he should make use of water.[13] I thought he was on the right lines.

If ever I felt desperate as a child and teenager, I would run and run and go to one of the two weirs close to our house and hear the rushing anger of the water, the gorgeous curve of it and the pound. I was comforted and grounded by the sense of danger. That done, I would wade into the river Frome from one of the little mud beaches I loved so much, hopping through the holes the cows had made when coming down to drink. I would feel the slap of water weeds around my calves, then thighs too, and sometimes I would press myself against the bank, pushing my arms hard back behind me, grabbing on roots, too deep, not steady, but enthralled by the water and its rapid movement. On it went. It didn't see me or care for me and that it could kill me without even knowing was a comfort: it made sense of how very tiny I was, and that, for some reason, made me feel safe. The roar of the weir was at my back, supernatural, and its volume made my anxiety and my cry small too.

I would go home, wet, calmer, and slope to my room, or sometimes curl into a ball in my den in the creepers. I remember being in year nine in secondary school and feeling a sense of separation and my oddity.

I was certain that no other fourteen-year-old in school curled themselves into a ball in a creeper den and wished

---

13. From *The Whitsun Weddings*, Faber and Faber, 1964: 'Water'.

themselves away. I was certain that no one else would have understood the weirdo pressed into the riverbank. What you do not know until you grow up a bit more is that the world is full of weirdos like you: water lovers, chuggers in the mud, wailers in the fields where the cows have been. That is an encouraging thought.

Herbs and bees therein. Escape

I am not alone and unacknowledged.

Bees are great, are they not? I sound like an excitable child, which, I suppose, I still am (and am glad!) Especially the handsome and voluptuous bumble bee. We need to do all we can to support them, of course, and that is why I have worked to mess up the garden around our family home, to make it into an untidy bee-loud glade. But to be honest and less kind, I wonder if it is also the idea, as before, of ridding a beautiful and (or) fascinating thing of difficult association. Because my father used to screech about bees. When he became ill and went mad, it got worse, and I found it terrifying because it was not explained to me and the things you do not explain to a child or a young person – even if your explanation is terrible – are the most terrifying things. Illness, death, and insanity are frightening for a child, but knowing that someone will attempt an explanation without overburdening you with information is and would have been key. Not, instead, that you will hear a hushed-up conversation behind doors which gives you an aw-ful feeling of something rattling towards you over which you have no control, which your peers are unlikely to know about and to which there is no assuaging comfort.

I remember once, during a panic in the car, he screamed about hell on earth. I had seen him as a strong man, physically robust, athletic, but never ill. He thought that he was in hell on earth and the traffic must have frightened him. Then there was a bee. My opinion was that it was a wasp, but as with not saying that a cormorant was, in fact, a shag in a previous essay in this book, one kept quiet. The bee/wasp skirted the windows and the ceilings, then made for him. I hated the idea that he would be hurt, but I was seventeen and was also scared, with no one to tell. He started shouting and wheezing and then whimpering in a high-pitched voice (I am paraphrasing), 'That bee! That bee! An end-time bee – it came for me! Why would it be in the car now? It is the bee sent from hell. The bee of Apollyon! There in the book: *The Book of Revelation*? Yes, isn't it? Isn't it? I am dead! Dead of abominations! God does not want me! Things are sent! It is too late!'

Wasp not bee, shag not cormorant, and in *The Book of Revelation*, it is locusts, not bees. Poor, poor thing. I held my breath, tried to make myself invisible because both my parents did not take comfort and would have baulked at it, even in a crisis, if I tried to offer it. I thought, *I am too sad to cry*. Now, we had pulled over to the side of the road, and Dad was screaming, 'Jesus, help me! Help me, Jesus! Come now and help me! The bee!'

I am not too sad to cry now. I cried when I wrote about this event, and I cried for my father. Because, really, he had gone mad. I cried because he had called for Jesus to help, and Jesus had not come in a way that was helpful, or appreciable, to him.

Now, I had always loved bees and even the danger of wasps. As a child, I felt sure that bees comported themselves in a gentle and gracious sort of way, but that wasps were born angry. One day a colony of digger bees[14] had arrived, would be there every year, making tiny molehills, then they disappeared. I was ready and waiting for that day because I loved to see their spiky energy and the way they hovered in a cloud together over the tiny tummocks they had built. Where they went, the year they did not return, I shall never know, but I hope they are bringing someone else joy or that their memory is. To this day, I will always try to put back to bed a bumble who has woken too early, knowing that it is unlikely to end well, but I will try. In our garden, I have planted as many bee-friendly plants as I can, and one of my favourite things is watching them hovering over beds of thyme in flower, the foxgloves, and the hardy geraniums. There is salvia everywhere too. I do sometimes think about my poor old dad when I see the bees, but mostly I watch their movement, and I think back to a time before the weirdness of the end-time bee; I let the tension in my body go – and, reader, things are such a trigger that this is necessary as a frightening possibility is that I will dissociate.[15] So I need other bee times as well as those associated with end times! Thinking back hard to days when I saw bees in clouds over shrubs and plants or when I saw the lollop of a bumble bee on a lawn and laid down to watch it, or sitting now with the creatures and trying to provide greater habitats for them, I am freeing them from an as-

---

14. Here is a book I love and which younger readers can enjoy, too. *The Little Book of Bees: An Illustrated Guide to the Extraordinary Life of Bees*, Hilary Kearney (author) and Amy Holliday (illustrator), Harper Collins, 2019. And as we are on this page, never forget to enjoy ivy, something we see everywhere and roundly ignore.

15. For clarification of what this can entail, I refer you to the NHS pages on the topic: https://www.nhs.uk/mental-health/conditions/dissociative-disorders/

sociation that is not good for me. Lavender (*Lavandula angustifolia*), Abelia (*Abelia grandiflora*), sometimes called the 'Bee bush' – honeysuckle (*Lonicera periclymenum*, the common honeysuckle and in the same family as Abelia), and I've let the ivy – there are two kinds, *Hedera helix* 'Goldchild' and 'Anne Marie' – run wild in part of the garden, knowing that it is a wonderful important late nectar source for honeybees and for queen bumblebees fattening up for hibernation, as well as the chosen pollen source of the solitary Ivy bee. Sedum – in our home, the large and pink blossomed *Sedum spectabile* (*Hylotelephium spectabile*), Autumn Joy – is great for them,[16] and there is an untidy rash of lungworts, *Pulmonaria officinalis*, about the garden. They are prolific self-seeders.[17]

So, I watch the bees, of many kinds, in our scruffy garden, and if an association comes, something frightening, I can tamp it down. It takes practice, but I can do it: or I sit as still as I can with the fear, but I think of it like Yeats's poem 'The Lake Isle of Innisfree' and its description of peace and what could be heard of the vestiges of that lovely thing even when somewhere less conducive to wellbeing. I think, *Ah, this is what I have tried to make or rather, this is what nature made around me*. I will be attentive, listen to the bees, study the lines of the bean rows I have made: I will look at what I have raised from the earth and regard lovingly what the earth tamped down.

---

16. Sedum is a large genus of flowering plants in the family Crassulaceae, members of which are commonly known as stonecrops. The genus contains a huge number of varieties, four to five hundred, by my understanding. You could make a sedum garden, use it for a green roof and have lots of specimens in pots in your house. It is, I think, one of the most cheerful and buoyant plants we have.

17. I love this plant's resilience and emerald, magenta, and amethyst colours, but I ought to say that it is toxic to animals and humans.

The whorls of new worlds. Detailed observance of the inner workings of complex flowers – and dissociation

To the body and mind which have been cramped by noxious work or company, nature is medicinal and restores their tone.

Once upon a time, I sat with a very depressed teenager after school and, drawing on my own experience, asked her if she might try to manage panic in the way I have done and still do, which is to observe things in minute detail. There were fuchsia bushes in the school border. 'I suppose.' I said, 'It'd be okay to take a flower and then afterwards, I will press it for you.'

That I did.

You could try this sometime, and it echoes what I have said in previous chapters of this book and will go on to say: observing the whole of something and then its constituent parts – you don't need to pick the flower because you could get down to the flower's level (if you can) and then just raise it up gently – looking step by step. The variety in question was a Fuchsia 'Tom Thumb.' I remember that the student told me she had never done this before; I reiterated that this was not something I knew as a professional in this area but that I had evolved for myself since childhood. So now, I must take you back.[18]

I do not know the exact circumstance under which we came to be here, but my parents attended a local book fair with an emphasis on educational books. I was with them, and I remember being told off because I had been too shy to talk to people. I was in primary school, nine years old. I felt ashamed because they told me I had shown them up. It hurts to write this, a small thing, but it felt huge because I *did* feel ashamed, and I have come to think that shame and humiliation are the precursors to or the bedfellows of depression. My mother said this often, and I felt I could tell no one because she would always add that it was obvious to everyone else and that she told other people, and they agreed, that my entire family agreed. I feel sad writing that, too, a little shivery because, to this day, I have uncomfortable feelings around my extended family, not because of them but because of what I ingested and took to be truth: words that came from my mother and to which my father acquiesced. Looking more positively, feeling those things is precisely why I always want to make sure that others I encounter have someone to tell and that if there is anything I can do, in however small a way, to help them have a voice, then please let me do it.

But let me take you back to that book fair, being shamed, and then a thing which happened because I came home with

_____

18. But not before this footnote! There are over one hundred varieties of fuchsia, and a fun fact tells us that a variety, *Fuchsia triphylla*, was discovered on the Caribbean island of Hispaniola (Haiti and the Dominican Republic) in about 1696–1697 by the French Minim monk and botanist, Charles Plumier, who became botanist to King Louis XIV of France and DID YOU KNOW that Linnaeus named a genus after him – *Plumeria*, or Frangipani, a bracelet of which I was wearing on the day I met my husband.

a book: it was the Piccolo Explorer Books *Guide to Wild Flowers*.[19] It was a small, slim volume, but I could not take my eyes off it because the illustrations were bright and alluring and there was something welcome in the font; it was large – not too large – and rounded. I loved the details and the scenes: Woodland Flowers, Hedgerows and Roadsides, Fields and Meadows, Heaths, Moors and Mountains – that chapter was how I knew what bilberries were because I once ran off on holiday, cramming my mouth with them before coming back to the car and a hard slap, the shame and sufferance (they were suffering *me*; before we went anywhere, my father would lean in and say, 'Remember you are only here under sufferance') talk and a couple of hours of stony silence – Seashore Flowers, Ponds, Streams and Marshes and Town Flowers.

I will tell you something else. I liked to order, label and sequence things. I longed to know the constituent parts of something – and still do. People made fun of it sometimes, but to me, it was and is a joy, though I was aware it did, in late childhood and teens, tip into a grim form of control. I will return to this later. But it was not that at first, and it is not that now. I am looking at the Piccolo *Guide to Wild Flowers* now. There is a picture of a meadow cranesbill in cross-section: stamen (anther and filament), carpel (stigma, style, ovary), petal, sepal (this was my favourite part because I *loved* the sound of the word), ovule, stem, bud receptacle and, of course, leaf and stem. I looked at this, pored over it time and again, and from that point onwards, I was hooked on looking at the constituent

19. *Piccolo Explorer Guide to Wild Flowers*, Michael Chinery, with illustrations by Ian Garrard, Piper, 1979. I believe this book is now out of print but accessible as a second-hand text. Another book pored over was *Wild Flowers*, Dietmar Aichele, with illustrations by Marianne Golte-Bechtle, Octopus Books, 1973, 1975.

part of flowers. Do you remember the depressed teenager I mentioned? I looked at a tiny flower with her now and named the parts. I said that even if you did not remember the parts, it was a fine thing to look at things, natural forms, all forms, in detail. For clear and delightful observance of the world, but also to ground you when you are scared, anxious, or your gloom will not shift. This is not professional advice, but something shared that works for me.

There's more because it was from this pretty guide that I learned the names of leaves and when I could not sleep, when intrusive thoughts came to stay, and ruminations were hard to manage – and I distinctly remember times alone in my bed when I was of primary school age, having to find ways to distract myself – I would say the words of the leaf arrangement aloud. Such as opposite, whorled, alternate and rosette. Then, I would think through the plants I knew and bring vivid pictures into my mind. I had been outside and looked at them so often, so tenderly, and I still do today: I would think of honeysuckle, rose, marsh pennywort, clover, wood anemone, frogbit. I could *see* them, *feel* them.

I have always felt that imagination is extraordinary and, at many times in my life, thought of it as substantial. Moreover, I have sometimes even wondered about the definition of real and imagined. Now my imagination was populated with some of the more common grasses, and, at night, I would count them like sheep: Meadow grass, Timothy grass, Couch grass,

Ryegrass, Meadow foxtail[20] – and on and on. Observance, names, and detail. *Always.*

Let me be your guide to wildflowers some time?

Back to the book fair.

The book fair took place was in a civic hall, and next door, people were giving blood. I remembered that detail, and I caught a flash of tube and bag. I was not scared, just fascinated, and it seemed like an excellent thing to do though it did get muddled up in thought, image, and impression in my head. I recall very clearly sitting there with the lovely book, looking at the backs of heads of two disappointed parents, knowing I was in for more talk of disappointment and would go to bed reflecting on how everyone in the room, all those bright and up and doing adults, must have seen what a drag I was on my exceptional family. In my thought was viscosity, carmine, doors softly closed and tubes and bags. I had a lively mind, and I think its weird cartwheeling saved my spirit on many occasions. There is something more, though. I went to give blood

---

20. Timothy Grass: *Phleum pratense* and known as cats' tails. This is a plant you see often and ignore. Next time, take a closer look at its beautiful and subtle colouration of greens and pinks. Couch grass, *Elymus repens*, is a bit of an enemy for gardeners because it has determined little rhizomes which spread and take over beds. Personally, I am fond of it for its determination, as I am of Ground elder. At home, I let it proliferate amongst the grass on the lawn, and it rejoices in the alternative name, Twitch grass. Perennial ryegrass is a tufted, vigorous grass of roadside verges, rough pastures, and waste ground. It is commonly used in agriculture and for reseeding grasslands, and, as with Couch grass, I loved its determination. Also, sometimes you see it as an annual and sometimes as a perennial. As if it were capricious. *Lolium perenne*; I knew that a translation of the second word meant everlasting, and this thought allayed my fear and nervousness. Finally, Meadow Foxtail is frequently confused with Timothy Grass, *Alopecurus pratensis*, but it is much bigger. As a kid, I knew it was a healthy food for invertebrates and a marvellous place to find caterpillars.

in the same place not so long ago. I eyed the door to the room where the book fair had been held, and as I sat there with my tea and a digestive biscuit afterwards, I thought only that if I were to take my three lads anywhere like the book fair and they did not speak as I had intended them to, or hold eye contact or do any of those things I got punished for, I would only say – this is assuming they had not been rude or revolting, as kids and young people can be (though adults, in my experience, much more so) – 'Were you a bit bored there, loves? Shall we go somewhere else now? And then I would tell them about my nature book, and they would groan.

Chastise your children but do not shame them again and again; do not tell them that all adults can see them for what they are because it is ingested and makes a child fretful and unsure of the world. Those children are pure gifts and did not ask to be born or brought into your family. They are as fine and miraculous as the constituent parts of a cranesbill or meadowsweet, such as a child might learn about in a beautiful book.

Dew on sedum. Finding comfort where there is none

Indeed the river is a perpetual gala, and boasts each
month a new ornament.

Do you know that the dew of the morning is the antidote to the damp and the mould of despair? The former is there, in a pearl, fine and beautiful in the eye of morning; the latter comes along, creeping overnight and if you turn your eye. An evil blue-grey velvet, echoing across domestic settings, and it says, 'Oh, little child, no one cares for you.' The pearl of dew? Ah, you see this perfect and transitory thing, and there is hope, suspended there. I love it best set in the firm leaves on my favourite sedum, *Sedum spectabile* 'Autumn Joy.'

Pearls of water. Crystal and white against the blue-grey of the sedum leaves, or there, looking it could be caught up and made into a brilliant by the most skilled jeweller: a permanent, multi-faceted diamond just waiting on the leaf of a climbing rose or even between the layers of rose petals in the Gertrude Jekyll which is thriving, its meniscus keeping it intact.

I think of something else when I watch for drops of dew on the lichen and moss on old walls here. Moss piglets, tardigrades, water bears: three names for tiny indestructible elements. We might see them in a droplet of water and, really, it is their planet, for there they have been thriving on moss and lichen, in the pretty bulbous drops of water on them, for 600 million years, preceding the dinosaurs by about 400 million years. Learning about these only recently felt hugely comforting. It was their very ubiquity: it is not as if, when you are sad, you can commune with the tardigrades, but their very abundance and proximity is, to me, gladdening. Also, that human beings are brief and outnumbered restores perspective, like climbing to the top of a hill and looking down with a bird's eye view is said to do.

I have always loved rain, too, and clouds (but that is a story for another book). The first little storybook I wrote was an account of raindrops, tiny perfect droplets on a classroom window when I was a kid. I named them all and imagined them as families, circulating their relatives time after time, telling stories, though I did not know what the stories were, only that they were there in a hieroglyphic language of which I could not account, and that was solace enough. I never wanted the answers: I wanted questions so big you could not possibly find answers.

Because I loved drops of water, I loved clouds. I was a cloud nerd and developed specific feelings about each to which I turn today. That is, I looked at each, identified them by name, thought about what they did – in case you had yet to realise, I love lists, names, and titles. Today, I have had therapy to deal with flashbacks and overwhelming feelings in body and mind, but I am not free of it. So, observance of pattern and the creation of it are useful for corralling my mind into calmer modes. Writing is excellent for that, too. But back to the list of clouds and writing about clouds!

Altocumulus. Patches and sheets; rounded balls of cotton wool. I enjoyed the variety in this one because it could be diffuse or tightly packed. Stretched fibres or rolled and balled sections. For me, the beauty of this cloud was not so much what it was, but its protean nature. All clouds are like this, but the altocumulus is most excitingly so for me. What had this to do with finding comfort or, at least, imagining it? Change. That change was possible, and things could move from one form to another or even in and out of form.

Altostratus. The rebel cloud; greyish or blueish. When I saw its curls, it reminded me of the shapes ice cream makes when you press and turn the ice-cream scoop. But then, ice cream reminded me of holidays, and holidays were a source of intense stress. It has taken me many years to free ice cream from this association and, likewise, the grand altostratus. We are not there yet, because memory and imagination are gorgeous but also capricious, and you cannot order them around as you might like. I remember a psychotherapist saying to me, 'But surely a tree is just a tree, at the end of the day.' I had two things to say to that. That no, a tree was not – at least for me – just a tree. It fared better if it were not a familiar tree of childhood and adolescence, but otherwise, a tree held memories, and shivers, and nightmares and scowling mouths and eyes. I say again and again in this book that part of my lifetime challenge has been to free gorgeous natural forms from association and live freely in them, just as they have been my blessing – a place of succour and locus of ideas.

Cirrocumulus. Ah, extraordinary sheets of clouds with the constituents arranged like grains or ripples. Even now, this spectacular sky seems granular and particular to me, solid, as if pieces of milky quartz were suspended there. I could make myself imagine that they sparkled.

Cirrostratus. This was and is a cradling cloud, its thin sheets sweeping across the sky and sometimes, if you were incredibly lucky, making a halo around the sun. As a child, you may see the natural world as benevolent, that it wishes to care for something or for you. I think that is how I characterised the cirrostratus.

Cirrus. I thought of this cloud as fingers to smooth my hair or a hand to gather me up in, sometimes as enthusiastic and joyous brush strokes. If I had to pick, this one is my surprising favourite because of its mischievous quality; now you see me, now you do not. I liked that. It was comforting because I imagined it as a discharge of energy, ideas, and joyful spirit right in front of me. When life is desperate, look to the sky.

Cumulonimbus. The mountain cloud, the thunderstorm cloud. Majestic, but I know I looked at these giants, and while they were clearly beautiful, they also heaped up, dark towns on a sad horizon. I have always loved thunderstorms, which they frequently presage, but love also comes by association. I do not really know why, but thunderstorms made my mother angry, and her anger, a bitter spite, gall, made me frightened. I feel unsettled even writing about that now. These days, I look at the cumulonimbus and try to free it from that association. Decades later, the delicious billow is still not free. It is like my mother controlled the elements.

Cumulus. A pillow, a hug. This is your classic fluffy cloud; although it's the cirrus, perhaps the opposite of the cumulus in form, I loved the pillow-like quality of this. When particularly tired or alone, I would always imagine jumping onto one; to me, they seemed the most substantial of the clouds. A place where you could go and reside if only you knew how.

Nimbostratus. The bad boy cloud and enough to block out the sun. Harbinger of rain or snow, and I loved this grey creature in both moods. One of my favourite things to this day is the nimbostratus, whose effect you feel and see: imagine the sun on your skin and light illuminating the sand. Then darkness and everything changes colour. This sudden shift is a moment of ecstasy for me in its drama. I also like sudden, powerful belts of rain,never more so than when I am by the sea. Standing in the water while being pelted – assuming you are not too cold – brings me to myself. For this reason, I associate this cross-looking cloud, quite contradictorily, with gratefulness.

Whether under clouds or a clear azure sky, though, drops of dew on sedum and rain of all kinds felt fresh and new to me and still do. That they are really old water, recycled again and again, and that when I stand in the rain and let it soak me, I am feeling something ancient that has travelled much, and known adventures I will never know is astounding. Below are the last two verses of a poem by the man who is still my favourite poet, George Herbert, 1593–1633. This is 'The Flower', a favourite of mine. Not long after we were married, I suffered a bad bout of depression, bubbling up after joy, and my new husband took me to places to distract and encourage me. One was the parish church of St Andrew's, at Bemerton, near Salisbury, which is a half-hour journey from where we live now. It was an extremely hot day – no rain then, but we are getting back to the subject and dealing with feeling, shall we say, parched – and I touched the tops of brittle, hot barley and wheat in the crop fields of the lower plain. I had a headache, so we walked down into the village and the tree-shaded lane, the cool church, which was George Herbert's first parish in 1629. Ned knew that I loved Herbert, and we had had a reading of 'Love' at our wedding those few weeks previously. In the church, we saw that the altar cloth had 'The Flower' on it: that poem has always seemed to me a supreme example of growth and wintering and renewal, and it is rich in its invocation of hydration, nourishment – a sousing by storm and a rehabilitation.

That was what I wanted. Ned instinctively knew, though, that I ought to see places and feel places and read words that would nourish and reorient my mind. When we married, I don't think he understood how deeply I had been damaged. We have been married now for twenty-three years, and still things are seen; a fragmenting. Or half-remembered things come out in nightmares: shapes, fear. This bout of depression had been triggered, I think, by difficult familial things which happened unchallenged at our wedding, and they cast me back to helpless childless days and, in my analysis of why I had had this reaction, I computed that if I could be insulted on my wedding day, it could happen anywhere. It had felt like an annihilation when a new relative openly criticised me as I left the church. I had been married for twenty minutes. Because it was my wedding day, I smiled on but was whirling about, wondering what to do or how I could call for help. Then, at my reception, an uncle, known to be difficult and surly but always excused, wished me well and then looked me up and down – bear in mind I am wearing a wedding gown, a tiara, and a veil – and then he tutted and made a theatrical sigh, saying, 'Oh dear. And your mother was *such* a wonderful woman.' I felt the panic rising. It is a trauma response, of course, and it comes back now: I am a child, scared, and there is nothing I can do. Also, my mother, though dead, will never leave me, and this is my punishment: for being a burden, a nasty little child, an eldritch creature, and a bringer of harm. The child, as I told you before, there in the most sublime, the best bee-loud glades, 'under sufferance.'

But now, it is a scorching day, and I am in the cool of a church, and I feel the water and read George Herbert, priest and of this parish.

> And now in age I bud again,
> After so many deaths I live and write;
> I once more smell the dew and rain,
> And relish versing. Oh, my only light,
> It cannot be
> That I am he
> On whom thy tempests fell all night.
>
> These are thy wonders, Lord of love,
> To make us see we are but flowers that glide;
> Which when we once can find and prove,
> Thou hast a garden for us where to bide;
> Who would be more,
> Swelling through store,
> Forfeit their Paradise by their pride.[21]

Will you forgive me some analysis here? So, Herbert sees God as Lord of power and Lord of love, constantly renewing the created world and the world of the human spirit. 'The Flower' is a poem of wonder and joy, but it does not stint in telling of darkness and depression, of despair and the isolation all those things bring. I had always loved the way I could hear – or thought I could hear – Herbert. He is a seventeenth-century priest and scholar, but his scriptural references are deft, gentle, and accessible, partly because they are so personal and contextualised in his own depth of feeling. He speaks inti-

---

21. *George Herbert The Complete Poetry* ed John Drury, Penguin 2015.

mately to me and to our own generation and those successive. 'The Flower' is, to me, greatly comforting, and in the sixth verse here, Herbert brings forward the recovery of the powers of creativity, a full restoration, and sense of wonder and incredulity that *I am he On whom thy tempests fell all night*. It is rain, storm, renewal: a livid and miraculous possibility, and it has always spoken to me of recovery. The poem's last verse shows where true happiness for human beings is to be found: not in trying to be what we are not or full of self-satisfaction, but rather in a truthful self-recognition and a clear-eyed sense of human mortality.

So that is the poem I was reading, from the altar cloth, while my head hurt and I battled depression. Will you think I am faking if I tell you it began to rain? I had not been paying any attention to the change in the weather outside, and I saw it was only a light shower, but I felt it on my bare upper arms and stood in it. You do not suddenly recover from a period of depression, but you can keep things in your store, I always found. The prickle-edged feeling of crops on Salisbury Plain, if you like, or the glint of that rain on dandelions around the old tombs in Bemerton Church. Or the lichen and moss, with drops of dew that hold a myriad of tardigrade,[22] here before

22. More on tardigrades! These were identified by the German zoologist Johann August Ephraim Goeze in 1773, who called them Kleiner Wasserbär – little water bear. Then In 1777, the Italian biologist Lazzaro Spallanzani named them Tardigrada, which translates as slow steppers. It is true; you will not see – although I am ready to be corrected – another phylum of eight-legged segmented micro-animals which are in less of a hurry. They have been found everywhere in Earth's biosphere, from mountaintops to the deep sea and mud volcanoes and from tropical rainforests to the Antarctic. As I said, they are among the most resilient animals known, with individual species able to survive extreme conditions – such as exposure to extreme temperatures, extreme pressures (both high and low), air deprivation, radiation, dehydration, and

you and here after you and yours and those who hurt you and loved you and the whole human race will be gone. All life is impermanent, and one day all the stars, Emerson's envoys of beauty, will go out, and the universe will, once again, go dark. Until then, a pearl of dew on sedum and a poem and a light rain are healing and a prompt to life enough.

---

starvation – that would quickly kill most other known forms of life. Tardigrades have survived exposure to outer space – or, as the astrophysicist Neil deGrasse Tyson says in *Cosmos*, they have been 'fired naked into space', which sounds more dramatic. There are about 1,300 known species. deGrasse Tyson also commented that an alien visiting Earth could conclude that this is the 'planet of the tardigrades' because these robust tiny creatures outnumber humans so vastly. I find thinking about them so cheering.

Vines and creepers, sea caves and hideaways. Finding new identity in secrecy

Nature is the symbol of spirit.

Here is a story about a six-year-old girl.

I do not remember exactly at which point it took hold, but I know that I was very young when I ingested the idea that everyone must think I was malevolent to people with heart conditions, pneumonia or those compromised by infarction, or that I had wickedly brought on others' ailments, disfigurements or sneezes by being this burden: the cruel little idea flew into my head and would not let go. And I thought that if I really tried to be less myself and more – I do not even know – floaty and insubstantial, then perhaps less harm could be done. Or if I really tried not to be me, really willed it, I could be someone radically different through magical thinking. I remember a specific time on holiday in our caravan (which my father loved and my mother hated): the sensation of the shiny, slipping velour bunk, the unfurled duvet. It was cosy in my little sleeping area, but it was also a place of retreat and change where, at night, I willed and willed myself to wake up as someone new. Because I knew about reading and how amazing it was, the imagination, metamorphosis in nature, I had an idea that in transformation through tenacity and imagination, I could wake up someone new.

But I could not and did not.

The heart raced: I would run outside at home. I would run into the woods. Now, while I was out there tree-hugging, might at least one person in the house die, and I would be found responsible, aged seven? What if other people would die because of things I did in times to come? To keep hidden from charge for a while I built a den inside the creepers near the beech tree, a crawl space. And, with a gentle, warm blush of light, I gave vent to my imagination and all the textures and smells of the den. I had several imaginary friends as a small child, one of whom was Frida from ABBA and another, Dolly Parton, whom I revere to this day. The den was really a crawl space, and no one could find me if I snuggled up inside, plus I had a big bag of Marks and Spencer tomato ketchup crisps, a pint of milk and a banana so I could stay fugitive for some time. There would be penance for the stolen food and drink, particularly the crisps, because my mother made special trips to Marks and Spencer for fancy crisps and walnut loaf because we had become middle class.

As a small child, whenever there was the possibility of making a den, a hiding plan, particularly a snug one, I would want to do it. When I had children, and they were young, I loved making dens about the house and outside, crawling into them, and recalling my own as a child. The difference was that, although I loved their building for their own sake, the impulse as a child to find, fashion and retreat was mingled with fear. I recall a particular time – this will sound bizarre as I recount it – when my father decided I ought to learn how to strike a match. What an odd memory. I was frightened of fire, but more specifically, the point at which the fire ignited, and I think, although I cannot be sure, that this might have been related to the number of bonfires my father had – a truly unnecessary number of bonfires, and sometimes in a very bad mood – and also because of the number of times we had chimney fires and the fire brigade had to come. It scared me, but I could not say. It was because he was performing a bonfire in the house and swept the chimney himself, but inefficiently. He was a practical man but had blind spots. So, I was terrified of the match-lighting episodes and ran. I spent hours in a crawl space, but not the usual one: this was a spot behind brambles and ivy in the wood by our house, and I crawled in sideways and laid down. I remember coming in when it was dark, and no one said anything, but at least the match lesson was over.

In all these places, there is so much observable detail if you really look. I counted what I could: ivies and Virginia Creeper; the puffs of Old Man's beard, cleavers with their tiny hooks which enable them to scramble – such resilience! – and the bindweed[23] that seemed to grow as you looked. From such a place, I could watch the wood anemones or bluebells.

But this was not all. Under sufferance – that is, with my parents, but ostensibly not *with* them, I would go scrambling and searching for hidden places on the beaches of Pembrokeshire. There is one cave on Newgale beach on St

---

23. Bindweed. It's terribly invasive but also rather beautiful, and I love its energy. *Convolvulus*: there are 200–250 species of it. As I said, it has energy, and I always enjoyed its confident, trumpet-shaped flowers. An underrated beauty in our too-tidy worlds. Virginia creeper rejoices in the name, *Parthenocissus quinquefolia*, Old Man's Beard is also known as Traveller's Joy, and its botanical name is *Clematis vitalba*; the common bluebell, *Hyacinthoides non-scripta* – my maternal grandmother called it a woodbell – and the wood anemone, a favourite of mine to this day, is *Anemone nemorosa*, one of the first spring blooms.

Brides Bay that you can climb through at low tide to cross between beaches and wade through at higher tides to access the
terrace of beaches cut off by the headland. When my mum
and dad were particularly angry with me, I would go crying
into the sea and walk for miles. I would always cross through
this beautiful cave because I thought of it like a lacuna: if I
went in one end, could I emerge the other end as something
better, acceptable. It was magical thinking. I would breathe
deeply, climb through and hope against hope. Sometimes I
would vomit: nothing had changed and my body was in rebellion. Still, as an adult, I saw this cave anew and now, when I
climb through it, I feel only the cold salt-smack embrace, and
its beauty. When I was younger, I used to look at other families playing beach croquet or boules and push on because I
had my cave; if I got through it and walked on, there were
further rough and shaggy cliffs to admire, few people about
even in the height of summer, and I could aim for the expanse
of shallow rock pools at the beach end: I would look up – I
could see sea bindweed, thrift and rock samphire – and down.
When I looked down into those pools, I used to count barna-
cles and sea anemones and hope for starfish and brittlestars
under the rocks, or myriad types of crab. They were tiny and
wondrous worlds, but there were also – and still are – a vehi-
cle for my imagination because I would think so hard about
the lives contained within, secreted under rock and wrack,
and imagine myself that small or just imagine them and be still
with it. That was a refuge, a kind of den, too: me and the rockpools, all alone. Or me, looking up, with the halophytes – isn't
that a beautiful word? – it means salt lovers, and I refer to the
plants that thrive in coastal areas: sea purslane, scurvy grass,
sea spurrey, glasswort, sea lavender and sea aster. I knew them
all in the lonely nerd-world.

So, I had the dens I built, or made, the cave, and I had my imagination; I could not tell anyone else because who would have listened? And anyway, I did not know how to describe what was wrong. I touched the rocks and the dry pebbles, looked at the shells wedged between the seams of caves and drew my fingers along them. I was caught between danger and rapture. I am writing this now, on a rainy day, in the small space in which I write, a desk, chair, and books cave, in front of a big multi-paned window. The rain is sweeping across the window, and I am looking at it on each small pain, a slightly different arrangement, and rain old as time; perhaps water I have met before because who knows? I feel safe and cosy in this little space as I write to you, but I also know that a memory may erupt with a thought or a word; I will receive an email in which the tone is unpleasant. That happens in publishing from occasional corners – I want to say this – and some of it almost stopped me writing. But I had friends to make me push through it because I have grown enough confidence to ask for help and not think I am dirt; or unworthy: not assume they will roll my eyes and think me stupid, weak, or indulgent, which was what I ingested year after year. And then, as now, I have or create these small spaces. Even in those I create, comes nature: in summer, the swifts in the eaves nearby, the pigeons roosting in the tree opposite – the elder tree that everyone counselled me to cut down but which is teeming with all kinds of life, as I knew it would be. When I see the pigeons lolloping onto the top of the elder tree, it is comical and comforting. They have a platform, a pigeon patio, because I grew an evergreen clematis, *Clematis armandii*, up the elder tree, and it is dense at all times of the year, sometimes with ivory and saffron-stamened flowers, at other times the fine lime-green bells of leaves that hide those flowers. What has this to do with a space, refuge or cave? I mean that these things enclose me, and I am deeply grateful; I will nurture them always.

On pressed flowers, pipe ends, bottle digging and the broken-winged dove. Walks in fields along hedgerows. Telling stories and easing lying nostalgia

*Visible distance behind and before us, is respectively
our image of memory and hope.*

If you were to excavate my house after my death, I regret to say that you would have thousands of books to move, sell or store. Not burn, for I should surely come back to haunt you. Excavate, and even then, do it with a light hand. Now I should add that it is not just the thousands of books, but what is within so many of them, the bigger hardbacks, mostly: sweet tissue filled with pressed flowers and leaves; sometimes, if I had been in a hurry, not a tissue at all, but just plants from garden and hedgerow hastily flattened with a thumb and a hope they would be desiccated enough and not lie there to moulder across the atlas.

This is not all of my keepsakes, because in little bowls and in printers' trays bought for a song are serried rows of foundlings: buttons, moustache combs, coins, pipe ends, pieces of old bottle from a Victorian bonfire and sometimes a glass stopper – a few lucky times, some beautiful pellucid glass stoppers from Anglesey or Dorset beaches, as well as the digs in old bonfires I remain so passionate about, there at the edge of fields and sometimes, if I could not resist after failing to find permission or footpath, a twilight incursion on the lip of a Wiltshire wood. Sometimes, extracted when the lias slipped and disgorged its old rubbish at Charmouth. With the flowers, the leaves, the glass, and other treasures, bowls of old pipe ends from Wiltshire and Somerset fields, picked up between the corn or, best, just after the corn was cut, and the soil turned and often brought home in great clarts of mud. Now and then, a pipe bowl, a gift, snuffed up and welcomed from old soil, jaggy hands and tired limbs which once had rested this way, and what did the smoker think?

What did I think now, looking at all these collectibles? I was often ill, that I did not understand how my childhood could be so full of extraordinary beauty and a terror I could not articulate. I went out one day in tears and hating where I lived for being too familiar and hating all the flowers and the things in bowls and printers' trays because they seemed so dull and unable to be freed from an association with my old immediate family, my now demolished home, and the stories I had tried to tell but could not, partly because I had been told that if they had been true, everyone would have known and seen. The old lie. This day, I had gone out hoping to see no one, and dusk was approaching. It was drizzling, and, with my hood up, isolation and that my embarrassment of tears could be concealed, were enough. The fields had been turned, and, as ever, I was eyes peeled and led by the nose, crunching over the stubble of the corn stalks. Eyes down, nose-led a small glow and a sharp edge.

Here was where I began questioning the provenance of the dove.

It looked at first like a chit of bone but, wiped off, it was something else. An ornament carved from ivory, a dove with one wing broken but otherwise perfect, raising up its remaining wing to fly high. The bird's head was drawn up, and the remaining wingtip keen and proud. Its wing was deeply carved, the shapes full of the mud of ages. I began telling stories, and here was a challenge. It was never entirely clear why, but because of a frightening past, growing up very rurally – although I suppose it would have been the same had I grown up around tall buildings and fast streets – I had learned to see everything through a gauze of something else. I could not see it freshly and imagine its former life for the first time, but instead through a piercing sadness with memories larded on, unwelcome and insistent. This is, I have since been told, the way of depression and perhaps of trauma too; the unbidden memory ushers in. So, when I looked at a view, a clot of red earth, the first celandines or flag iris, there was the challenge, and here it was now. Holding the little ornament, I tamped down visions of the little presents from my parents; tiny pottery animals: pretty and snug in the palm of your hand, but always, beyond, the sense that you were unsafe and if you put a foot wrong (which you so often did), a beating with a hairbrush, a handful of hair or the words and the assurance that all those you knew or would know would think you the same fool as those who knew you best.

But here was determination, and I wonder if it is strongest in those who are repeatedly told they should not survive or deserve to, who are told it would have been better if they had not been born. Close a hand over the dove and construct a story, sui generis: what was the provenance of the dove? It did not seem like something a child would have lost in a field, though it might have been something burned long ago, then

73

bleached again in the sun of field turnings and heavings. Was it something that a man working in the field 150 years ago had given to his sweetheart? Where might he have got it? Was it bone and not ivory? Had she received this token and then lost and cried? Worse, had she rejected a loving man and the dove been deliberately lost, thrown into the field by him or by her? I wondered if, more prosaically, it had simply been worthless rubbish to someone and burned there at the edge of the field, integrated into the furrows, seeing the light over a century, then the darkness again. I decided here was my story: a man loved a woman and gave her a perfect white dove. By accident, she dropped it and could not find it; she never told him, and he loved her, how he loved her. It was buried, being found many years later by someone who thought it lovely and carried it home to a family where it was enjoyed and wondered at and placed in a printer's tray, the earth still adhering. 'No,' said my eldest son, 'Put it on the windowsill outside where everyone can see it. It wants to be in the light again,' and his words gave freshness and freedom to the dove and to me.

That day, I looked at the many books full of pressed flowers, too. I had love in the mist and sepia-tinged camellias and lavender, but most of all, the hellebores[24] that, as a child, I knew only as Christmas roses. My mother had an upturned fridge drawer over a loved and cosseted flower, and I was told never to touch the covert; often, I could not even see it because the clear plastic was covered in condensation, so it was a mystery plant and, because I did not know anything of the hellebore, I thought it was a rose that knew only to flower at

---

24. *Helleborus niger* is the hellebore in question, but the Helleborus gang consists of approximately twenty species of herbaceous or evergreen perennial flowering plants in the family Ranunculaceae. I love every one of them and search out hellebores wherever I am.

Christmas. It was strange: once, she allowed me to see it, on a cold November, and there was just one little bloom, cream and jade-hued and the tiniest hint of carmine. I did not understand. She said, 'It will not last until Christmas', and I know that I was unutterably sad. I had many piercing memories like this: of mysteries and people going away and beautiful things not coming to fruition. I did not know, then, that not all lives were this melancholy or all children this sad. When I was older, I remember understanding that there was more than one hellebore and that I had to free myself from their association with this delicate and damned flower of my childhood. I grew them, and they were big and blowsy; I had them in my wedding bouquet, and, in the Deep South of my husband's family, they grew in forests and were in bowls by my bed. All kinds of them – and ones that looked just like the friable baby in the upturned fridge drawer.

Now my cookbooks and an atlas or two are full of pressed hellebores, and when I touch them or just greet them forgetfully as I open a book, I know that the Christmas rose of my childhood home was also something else: a focus for sadness, something to cosset which, from cosseting and being brought on out of season did not thrive and I feel sad for that mother whom I feel I hardly know or knew. But I do not feel sad for the hellebores, rampant outside and living again in my books, blooming without attention, tears or melancholy, year after year.

You will see some if you come to visit me, as I hope you will, several varieties bountiful opposite a window on which ledge there are fragments of sea glass, a dove with a broken wing, and a flotilla of pipe ends. And they are not reimagined things of the past, but their own kind, sui generis, so I can look at them without melancholy or a tilt towards the fear and cold fury of my childhood which to this day rise up and make me so unwell.

Sui generis,

Helleborus.

Hello, hope.

I want to tell you more about collectibles, but when I was younger, they became a mixed blessing because the joy of putting things together – *for me*; please do not read and assume this is necessarily a conduit to psychological peril: only that there was a link of some sort for me[25] – at some point, stopped being lovely and became a compulsion. And with it, I remember the awful ruminating thoughts, the intrusions into a blue-sky day coming like a dark punch. It was frightening. I had thoughts, which are explored elsewhere in this book because they're a key part of my experience, of being a bringer of harm. I was convinced that I had been violent, caused risk to other children or spoiled things for them, though if you had asked me, I would not have been able to explain why. I feel a shiver writing that now. Why?

Because the thoughts and proclivities have echoes.

What began in childhood, with checking and symmetry and hoarding of lots of little things I did not want and deep anxiety about preserving and curing things in nature – I will return to this – reappeared with full force when I became very ill about ten years ago. Then, I arrived at therapy and told the psychologist about the re-emergence of these feelings. I explained that my mother had said I had brought on deaths, that

_____

25. Because the term OCD seems to be used flippantly and far too much, I would argue, I offer a resource here. https://www.ocduk.org/ocd/ It does not mean someone who's fussy about their beans touching their mashed potato or who has a particular yen for straight hems or sequencing.

I had made my father worse and failed to understand, that another person had told me I had shortened their lives and that the entire family was aware of this, and that, some years before, a girl in my school year had died and I had become convinced I was linked because, when we were five, I had encouraged her to jump and she had fallen and cut her head, then said I pushed her and told everyone. My parents had not believed me, and decades later, my mother said I should not send a card after she died in case the family held me responsible in some way.

I told all this: I told the therapist in between choking, wrenching sobs about it. I told her about my collectibles and how it all became about symmetry, shades, hues, and that, if they were not right, awful things would happen. We worked hard, then, on letting the thoughts flood my head and feeling what it did to the body, then noticing, in this soothing and safe environment, that nothing else had happened or had ever happened. This was (partly) the way we re-trained me in which the fear diminished.

In my childhood bedroom had been 'The colour table' and 'The rules of the room'. The table was visible, and the rules were not. I changed the colour table weekly: a polished stone, a rosy cameo brooch of uncertain provenance, a scallop shell with a rim, and some damask flower petals. I always formed navigable gaps between them. So that, if you were *really* small, say, you could walk along the little roads between the petals of an aster and the cameo brooch. This was the secret bit: the colour was pleasing to any onlooker, but the order, traced round and round in the curlicues of a little finger – of my little finger – was the private bit. It may appear to you, reader, that this was an overly detailed way in which to see something; or a recollection that cannot possibly be. But it *was* and *is* so. Such a commanding impulse: to arrange little things in groups and trace a finger round the gaps in between, a microcosm that is intimate and seen only by its author. And when the impulse tipped, or when it all became part of something else, a compulsion, it was so bad. I felt I had to continue because something would happen. Truly, I don't know how, without familial support, I managed. I hope it will have been or will be vastly different for you, lovely reader.

Today, if I press flowers, though they can be imperfect, the shiver I just told you about has passed. It gets weaker and weaker over time, but I must be careful. Two years ago, away from home, a person looked at me hard and told me some home truths and told me some home truths about our children; there was something in it which was so familiar. A flashback. I wandered the rented house at night, crying, shaking. But I looked at the stars, the Plough, Cassiopeia's chair, and found comfort. I thought I could not die because the stars, these envoys of beauty, were there, as they had always been. I could carry on, as I had always striven to do. The next day, I burrowed my feet in the sand and walked luxuriously in the sea and though the things lingered, and the voice said more words about me and about my children, in the bright of day and the ardent beauty of the soft things and warm things in the natural world about and in the sheer scale of the Atlantic stretching out beyond me, on and on, I found perspective and easement. Do you know what else I felt? Anger.

Anger is good. Rage. Fury. As it rose, I shouted into the sea: bellowed. The sea met me benign, disinterested. The sea is used to that sort of thing, and anyway, it did not have time. It has been so helpful for me to think of this, of vastness and how that sea just there, the North Atlantic, pressed on to the Atlantic far away and the Southern Ocean and spanned out to the Pacific and the Indian and way above to the Arctic. I put my rage into that sea, and it carried it out, uncaring, and broke it up, and it was dissolved.

On lichen and moss. Patterns, fractals, futures, grief, and survival

Every natural fact is a symbol of some spiritual fact.

In nature, there are things which have grown to look like each other and yet are radically different, living side by side. I loved it when I learned to tell the difference and found it liberating, both because of the majesty of the facts involved and because of my weird and allusive little mind, I saw, recalling the Emerson quotation in this chapter epigraph, the natural fact as a symbol of some spiritual fact. So, I saw range, dynamism, mystery, and comfort. Lichen and moss could be observed together in the woods in which I ranged – several of which I ought not to have been in – and the walls I looked at.

Both mosses and lichens are considered non-vascular plants, but only mosses are truly plants. Lichens aren't plants at all; instead, they are complex organisms formed by a symbiotic relationship between a fungus and an algae or cyanobacteria. They are huddled up together like the best of friends and still radically different. Within the lichen, there is symbiosis – something else which grabbed me early. It meant what it meant, but perhaps, the allusive little mind thought, it meant something else: about heaven, or God, or the world, or what people would learn to do if they would only read nature. I read there were several types of *mutualism* – a mutually beneficial symbiotic relationship, commensalism – a one-sided symbiotic relationship, parasitism – one species lives on, in or with a host species, competition – a relationship in which organisms compete for resources, and predation and herbivory – symbiosis where one organism feeds on another. I loved finding that out, and while I understood that these things were all about balance within an ecosystem – weirdly, I showed no promise in science at school, but I think this was because I hated it all, felt unsafe and had my home science thoughts and books and my nerd-mind – I liked the idea of the mutually beneficial relationship best, and I liked to see plants together, like the moss and the lichen on walls.

Both are sturdy and were here before us and will be here after us, one would think. That scale of my and our very impermanence has always been comforting. Recently, I have been observing lichen because I realised I could not name it in its myriad varieties; on recent walks, I found and named ten varieties, seven of which I found in an old wood. The common orange lichen or yellow scale (*Xanthoria parietina*) was spectacular, but my favourites are the modest grey and silver-green of Monk's Hood lichen (*Hypogymnia physodes*) or that my paternal grandfather called (he went poaching pheasant, so spent plenty of time in the woods), 'grey knot.' As a child, out rambling alone, I thought they were sneakier and more secretive the duller their colour, but I enjoyed them all, rubbing my hands on tree trunks and prodding dead wood on the ground. And feeling the bounce at my fingertips – or heels – of the moss that was soft to the touch and which softened my world.

So, I used to think about the sturdiness of these things and our impermanence. I would ponder their resilience and lose myself in them. Most of all, it was a special and private habit of observance because I found that people like bright flowers and great structures, but, at least in *my* childhood sphere and adult cohort, moss and lichen nerds were short on the ground.

Now, what about patterns? In adulthood, we have yet to find – although *I* think it is obvious: my immediate family largely detested me – the underlying cause of what I imagine is complex PTSD. So, while my medical notes of, say, the last couple of decades will tell you that the hospital psychotherapist wrote down 'complex trauma,' and the recovery bit of mental health services, similar things and everyone else low mood and depression, I do not think we are there yet. As a side note, we would be more *there* had not primary care lost several years of paperwork, which only became known recently. I am so sorry if this discourages anyone reading this for whom mental health problems are ongoing or assumed better, but you see, it is stop-and-start, for me, imperfect. This is okay. Still, yesterday, a sweet WhatsApp message from a family member with good intentions and kindness sent me into a spin. Just news about extended family events and the sibling with whom I have no contact, an anodyne message. But still. I read it, then felt a creeping fear come up from my toes: it is like dark water or a smothering silence is going to cover me, and I have felt it for years and years. Then, as if I were back in the moment, as if I had never left, a fear and a vulnerable child with laughing and derisory faces about me.

Do you see how I try to give it shape and name? That has always been vital, and my love of the natural world and passion for reading have helped with this, too. Because it is chaotic, what bubbles up. A flashback. You know you are not there and, rationally, cannot be demeaned or even annihilated. Your rational brain, even as all this is going on, knows it to be the case, but all the rest of you is shaking with it, querulous and saying, please do not. Then, as I begin to emerge from the alternative reality into which I deep-dived, I see the objects around me and feel that they are separate, known but unknown. I feel like I am above me, next to me; I do not know where my edges are, and, on the worst occasions, I am not sure who I am. What a busy brain.

Will I ever be better? I think probably not, but I am, during the composition of this memoir and thinking about everything that has gone and my methods, as well as my intense loves now – for the lines of a plant, the edges of rime on a gate – *all* of these wonders, these things so much their own and these envoys of beauty – I *am* investigating how we go forward, so I am not propelled into flashback and dissociation by news, being misrepresented, having my story mistold and the hard shapes of an unkind look on a face which frighten me in a way which is enfeebling; excessive.

I turn to a pattern in happiness and living with this fear. What I can observe and what I can make. Yesterday, I was looking at lichen and moss, the way they were snuggled together on the bug logs I have stacked around the garden. Then, I was thinking about symbiosis. Today, after yesterday's blueshift,[26] where I felt chaos erupt around me, I thought of fractals.[27] Fractals in the natural world are patterns that the laws of nature repeat at different scales. I have always found I

---

26. I sometimes comfort myself by reading scientific papers, and a particular area of interest is astrophysics. In addition, I think of scientific concepts – particularly within physics – as a way to describe feelings and symptoms. I appreciate some of you will think I am weird. Here is a description of red and blue (or negative red) shifts. https://ned.ipac.caltech.edu/help/zdef.html

could get lost in them, and that what I could not see, I would imagine hard. When I was not counting sheep at night, I was counting fractals. So now, I think about emerging ferns or succulents when I feel scared and find their coils and corners and pull of infinity immensely grounding, if that is not too dull a term for something so miraculous. You can see them in plants and other organisms, in mountains, in earth and in sky. The nautilus shell: perfect and pristine. I did not find one but was given one found by my husband's grandmother. It is a Fibonacci spiral, and maybe the simplest way to describe this is that this shell is a self-similar curve which keeps its shape at all scales. As a child, I tried and tried again to capture snowflakes under the microscope but had to settle for watching the snow. So, I was overjoyed to discover the catalogues of W.H. Bentley, whose work is referred to elsewhere in the book.[28] They are fractals, repeating, for me – this may not be so for you – something so incredible that I could not observe them without thinking they were not only themselves but had symbolic value; a language we could not understand: a manifestation of the divine, which was something that Bentley thought about too. How about lightning, broccoli (*Brassica oleracea*)? – particularly the Romanesco, an astonishingly symmetrical fractal, Queen Anne's Lace (*Daucus carota* – sometimes called Wild Carrot) with its layers of delicate, iterative

27. *The Fractal Geometry of Nature*, Benoit Mandelbrot, Cambridge University Press, 1982. This is a gorgeous and fascinating book on the topic. Mandelbrot defines the fractal as 'a rough or fragmented geometric shape that can be split into parts, each of which is (at least approximately) a reduced-size copy of the whole.'

28. *The Snowflake Man: A Biography of Wilson A. Bentley*, Duncan Blanchard, Macdonald and Woodward Publishing Company. 1998. Contains astonishing photographs of snow crystals – photomicrographs – collected by Bentley in his Vermont home.

blooms, ferns, the foot of a gecko, a pineapple. When I could not be with these things, then as now, I would look for images of them. The tail of a peacock! Stalagmites and stalactites – I have always loved caved and could stare at these for hours – crystals, coastlines, sea urchins – I have collections of sea potatoes, medium-sized urchins, washed up empty on wintry Pembrokeshire beaches – starfish, rivers and fjords, a careful and unhurried examination of the underside of a leaf or the pattern of a tree's branches. They are everywhere. So there: companionable plants, symbiosis, patterns, fractals. It is not that they were and are a cure, but they are part of one and a stabilising influence throughout my life. I have always made collections of similar things, too, from white-ringed grey pebbles to hagstones, which are pebbles with a hole in them, to feathers, cones, and leaves. Our home is full of repurposed jars and tins and baskets with these things in them, and, when I have time, I might assemble things into patterns and place them in plaster, a pebble ammonite preserved for my children; comfort for them, too?

To return to 'Snowflake Bentley', a phrase comes to mind, and it is Bentley, puzzling over the extraordinary design of snow crystal. Bentley was aware that the structure of crystals changed with temperatures as they fell through the atmosphere, but this description is of reading them – and I think this is what I have tried to do, particularly when my mind could not cope, when I was at sea. I look for patterns and try to think of the story and the wonder compact with that. A careful study of this internal structure not only reveals new and far greater elegance of form. Bentley *read* the stories of snow crystals, thinking how, in their wonderfully delicate and exquisite figures, much could be learned of the history of each crystal and the changes through which it had passed in its journey through cloudland. He thought it was as if a life history had been written in 'dainty hieroglyphics' and imagined a momentous journey as he read that history. And all of it was secret until you seized the moment while the crystal was intact and *looked*.[29]

I love the idea of secrets hidden in plain sight. A little while ago, I discovered the works of Thomas Merton and read *The Seven Storey Mountain*.[30] I was fascinated by his description of entering the supernatural life of church, that he both became both a new man *and* remembered who he was – a beautiful and lingering paradox – and, most of all, his description of the miracle hidden in plain sight. Merton told of how life is so simple, that we are living in a world that is transparent, with the divine shining through it all the time. That description was and is thrilling to me. I have kept looking, and I am still looking, but truly I feel something pulsing and biting in life and never more so than in solitude in nature.

I have never got on well with church because my experience of it has so much to do with warring factions, dislike of children, bitterness and the oddness of diocesan activity, which seems, to me, too often to be radically disconnected from faith and predicated on a climb to success, on being religious, seen to be religious and seen to be staying religious. I do try, and I do read, think, and pray. But most of all, it is when I am alone, unfettered, that I feel that pulse and that bite and am swayed by so much Merton has written. So, you see, the natural world is *that* for me, too: there is the teasing possibility

---

29. *The Snowflake Man: A Biography of Wilson A. Bentley*, Duncan Blanchard, Macdonald, and Woodward Publishing Company. 1998, pp.51.
30. *The Seven Storey Mountain: An Autobiography of Faith*, Thomas Merton, Harper One, 1999. The original text, sometimes described as a modern-day Confessions of St Augustine, was published in 1948.

of things tapped out, symbols, secrets, in shapes and forms all around us, beauties we did not make. We may know the language, the semiotics, is there but cannot read or interpret it proficiently. But more than that, I feel and hunger for vastness, wilderness, wildness, and the notion of something supernatural that we are too small to read.

When people say they need evidence to understand fully and therefore be able to believe something, I am baffled. I do not *want* to fully understand because my understanding is and will always be too small. I want to be dazzled, at least in part, by incomprehension and enormity of scale. It is enough for me to *try* and understand and to feel. To think that something divine is shining through and that the world is not murky but transparent; there, numinous on the darkest and most raging sea.

If you are a trauma survivor, you may go on to lower your expectations of the world of other people. I have certainly found it difficult to trust adults and now, grown up, other adults, but at no stage have I ever thought less of God or, for that matter, of the common primrose on which I cried hot tears – or the snow I held in my hands and loved, just as W.H. Bentley did.

In praise of holding and being held by trees. Wishing trees, dens, hollows, and dead wood. Fear and its assuaging

Space, time, society, labor, climate, food, locomotion, the animals, the mechanical forces, give us sincerest lessons, day by day, whose meaning is unlimited.

In the long and straggling wood attached to our house, there was a tree, and this was a tree I always loved. I loved all trees, but this one had a particularly strong personality and something within it which offered comfort. It was a beech, and I see that The Woodland Trust has this to say about the common beech, which is anything but: it is 'Monumental, majestic, home to rare wildlife. Beech is an enchanting species and known as the queen of British trees. To wander beneath the leafy canopy, its cathedral-like branches spreading upwards, is an awe-inspiring experience.' All of this. *Fagus sylvatica, my Fagus sylvatica*, had a smooth bark I would hold my cheek against, lukewarm and giving. It had a kind of firm foot to one side, where the trunk curved out into the soil, so there was a gentle child-sized slope to stand on; from my purchase here, I would climb onto the tree and wrap my arms around it tightly. I would whisper to the tree and make a wish, which usually involved being a long way away or in this beautiful place but feeling safe. If I wished to think hard about travel, well, I had already stepped aboard the tree, slightly above the earth, so my imagination needed only take a short step before we were airborne, flying to families of beech all over the world. Perhaps the more demure *Fagus grandifolia* in North America, the small American beech. I'd looked them all up, inventing a family for my own beech and thinking that, as I whispered to the beech, the beech whispered to its cousins and, perhaps, shared my whispers, and I was less alone.

Frequently, I did not feel safe growing up. Even writing this, I do not feel safe because those feelings ebb back. As far as I understand it, I have developed around an uncertain core, so while I have done my best, with latter-day therapeutic support, to bed in new ideas, if my senses taste something bitterly familiar, back it floods in. This is a time when an intimate encounter with plants or natural phenomena is salve, speaking a language which is safe and true. There is more, because just as I looked at the bold fuchsia of the Rosebay Willowherb and felt a lift in my spirits, I sometimes see the forms of the natural world as metaphor for something larger and so much better. I mean that each striation or delicate whimsy in a plant is like a word or an idea. I cannot read it, but metaphor may connote something we can only begin to grasp at, numinous and redolent of such hope. Fireweed; fuchsia: intemperate straggling plant. What might it say if one day I understood? What of the solidity of the beech tree and, if I concentrated extremely hard, the delicate fluctuations in texture, temperature even (I was so certain I felt it, like a pulse!) What if it told of clues to a greater and everlasting wood, and this place was my church? That is how I feel around trees, and when I go into an old church, I feel as much pull of faith in the moss and lichen of a wall as kneeling by an altar cloth.

I think of my wishing tree often and of sailing in it. I do not know if it is still there because, when my childhood home was bulldozed, it made way for something more gracious and symmetrical, as someone took the ramshackle bungalow in the vast garden and built up and out. When they had made a neat and bold house for themselves, they razed the old orchard and scraped a fine drive out of the wild wood and landscaped the gardens into tidy terraces and hid areas with *Leylandii*. Perhaps the wishing tree is there, but it was curved and untidy, and in the subjugation of nature, this will not do. But there are times when I squeeze my eyes shut and pretend I am squeezing the wishing tree. I am crying as I open my eyes, but the tree is in front of me, pellucid and bold, asking me what I wish for and where I want to go today before it fades and is gone.

I want to tell another part of my story here.

I would often plan to escape. When I was very young in the way that stroppy children do, but even while I was in years four and five in primary school, I kept recalling a phrase in Beatrix Potter's *Pigling Bland*[31] about how, if you cross the county boundary, you could never return. That is what I had in mind: our house was in Wiltshire, but our garden was in Somerset, so when I told you in the introduction that I lived

_____

31. *The Tale of Pigling Bland*, Warne 100th ed. Edition, 2002. The book was originally published in 1913. 'if you once cross the county boundary you cannot come back' and '...they hurried downhill towards the county boundary... They ran, and they ran, and they ran down the hill, and across a shortcut on level green turf at the bottom, between pebble beds and rushes.

They came to the river; they came to the bridge – they crossed it hand in hand – then over the hills and far away she danced with Pigling Bland!'

on the boundary, I really meant it. And I knew where other Wiltshire–Somerset borders were, and I also had in mind the Severn Bridge and crossing into Monmouthshire, Sir Fynwy. I would idle away times of wakefulness late at night, planning which county – or country – boundary I would cross and how, in daring, I would never come back.

I had my books, maps, roads, and fields in my imagination. I plotted it all and thought about what to take. I was bold, and I was alive, and I was going to say goodbye to this beautiful place and find some other people who would want me just as I was. Oh, but so sad: the spirit of that dare did not sustain me, and I remember that, instead, I was claimed by crotchety leonine summers and then by damp autumns and snarling winters: they were colder inside than out; even the radiators managed to radiate cold. Silence sat over the house; everything began with a closed door. I would scamper in – determinedly larger than life and determined to be helpful. Trying to be that thing they wanted, but what did they want? Impossible, of course: riding the skirts of my father's stress, watching the pulse throb angrily in the temple as he cooked (for which he had no natural talent) as my mother laid in bed. I would endeavour to boil potatoes, make tea, and end up making an enormous mess. It brought only a shout and a child rushing out to the beech tree – the wishing tree in the wood, with its kind heart and tender trunk.

'Get out, you little cuss. You always make everything worse!' shouted my father. I wanted to see my mother but was told I'd make her more ill. I think, like many children, I just needed to be held, so instead, I would run out to the wood, and the banging of pans would diminish. I would wrap her arms about the tree's velvet neck and say, 'Make me fly!' Or 'Make

d. I was depressed in childhood and can feel that on
ow. I see that kid and want to go back and give her
would for my own children. What happened when
ay? The responses were gentle but disbelieving,

e has put that in your head
chobabble
ere and would have known
e never mentioned this before
anselling has put ideas in your head
else is saying these things

tried to talk about how I had been frightened of
, it was cut short. She was someone else's mother,
nd, and colleague, and to the world, she was mar-
e was those things, too and while a therapist might
sted there were conversations to insist on, I did not
only harm could be done. But you see, I was fright-
mother. As I grew older, less frightened of what
lo to me physically, impulsively, because I got big-
r, and her health, never good, got worse. She was a
person in so many ways, and so was my father, so
t be that I felt these things? It takes a long time to
a start, if your childhood contains a lot of uncom-
lings and you are often scared, this needs the in-
nt or carer to unpick and lead to appropriate care.
t be incumbent on the child, young and vulnera-
h scant experience of the world, to sort it out. If
quently feels ashamed or dirty, and has repeated
(that extend, with an experience of choking, into
then there was something wrong. What possible
d there be for you to make it up and somehow
workings of your body so that, with a variety of
pulse quickened, and you felt cold and clammy?

me just me and free!' 'Make me a tree!' Or just, 'Make me not
be.'

But whatever happened, whatever I said and however
much I cried, the beech tree with its base like a long heel
I could step onto was there, and it thought, if a tree ever
thought, that this kid was okay.

I will always be grateful to my *Fagus sylvatica*.

Of kelp and the stories it pro
sharp company when frighter

The wheels and s[
hypothesis of the perr
built like a ship to be to:

I will take you to kelp and salt b
dreams.

From my earliest years, or ratl
member, I felt a sort of screamir
make sense, but it existed. I thoug
foundly wrong with me even as ;
have had the vocabulary to exp
now: because there was kindness
I met kind people in the extende
had failed them. How could I be
I was given birthday presents or
me to the beach at night, and I la
the salt swell? Surely, I had misin

There was a time in my twer
some members of my extended fa
with me and how I had been repe

and beyo
my pulse
a hug, as
I tried to
Some
It is p
I was
You h
That
Nobc
Whe
my mot
sibling,
vellous.
have su
agree. I
ened of
she wor
ger tha
wonder
how co
unpick
fortabl
put of
It shou
ble an
the chi
nightn
adulth
reason
manag
stimul

me just me and free!' 'Make me a tree!' Or just, 'Make me not be.'

But whatever happened, whatever I said and however much I cried, the beech tree with its base like a long heel I could step onto was there, and it thought, if a tree ever thought, that this kid was okay.

I will always be grateful to my *Fagus sylvatica*.

Of kelp and the stories it provides. Salt, ancestry, and sharp company when frightened of rejection and anger

The wheels and springs of man are all set to the hypothesis of the permanence of nature. We are not built like a ship to be tossed, but like a house to stand.

I will take you to kelp and salt by way of fear and feelings in dreams.

From my earliest years, or rather from the earliest I can remember, I felt a sort of screaming fear in my ear. It did not make sense, but it existed. I thought there was something profoundly wrong with me even as a small child, but I must not have had the vocabulary to express it. I am pondering this now: because there was kindness too and books, and because I met kind people in the extended family, I would feel like I had failed them. How could I be carrying these feelings when I was given birthday presents or when an aunt and uncle took me to the beach at night, and I lapped up the magic and loved the salt swell? Surely, I had misinterpreted?

There was a time in my twenties when I tried to talk to some members of my extended family about feelings I carried with me and how I had been repeatedly ill in my teenage years and beyond. I was depressed in childhood and can feel that on my pulse now. I see that kid and want to go back and give her a hug, as I would for my own children. What happened when I tried to say? The responses were gentle but disbelieving,

Someone has put that in your head
It is psychobabble
I was there and would have known
You have never mentioned this before
That counselling has put ideas in your head
Nobody else is saying these things

When I tried to talk about how I had been frightened of my mother, it was cut short. She was someone else's mother, sibling, friend, and colleague, and to the world, she was marvellous. She was those things, too and while a therapist might have suggested there were conversations to insist on, I did not agree. I felt only harm could be done. But you see, I was frightened of my mother. As I grew older, less frightened of what she would do to me physically, impulsively, because I got bigger than her, and her health, never good, got worse. She was a wonderful person in so many ways, and so was my father, so how could it be that I felt these things? It takes a long time to unpick. For a start, if your childhood contains a lot of uncomfortable feelings and you are often scared, this needs the input of a parent or carer to unpick and lead to appropriate care. It should not be incumbent on the child, young and vulnerable and with scant experience of the world, to sort it out. If the child frequently feels ashamed or dirty, and has repeated nightmares (that extend, with an experience of choking, into adulthood), then there was something wrong. What possible reason could there be for you to make it up and somehow manage the workings of your body so that, with a variety of stimuli, your pulse quickened, and you felt cold and clammy?

Here comes a memory of a secondary school Maths teacher who knew my parents. He shamed me in front of a year 9 class. Said that my parents were wonderful and had such high hopes for me and *look at the wet and spineless thing* I was. I struggled with Maths; I struggled with everything. How could I explain this and have it believed? Again, from my form tutor: *they are such good people, and you must be such a source of stress to them.* I want to say to any teacher reading this: do not be fooled; do not always believe the adults, and please: try to understand that someone can be kind in some spheres, a beacon, and not fit for purpose in another. Human beings are not dreary binary objects, no, no: they are never so.

Once, at lunchtime, I ran out of school and sat under a big oak tree in a field on a hot day. The only way to bring me back to myself was the sun on my neck and the kind branches of that tree. I remember that I went back in, feeling like there was a dreadful emergency, but how could I ever communicate such a thing? I had wanted to die very badly. Or rather, I screwed my eyes up hard and wanted not to be. If this was and is ever you, do this for me: screw your eyes up under an oak tree or that tree in your imagination, and then get up and run into the world with rage, with compassion in your heart because you know, don't you, that this is not fair, and you do not want anyone else to feel this lonely. There is a choice: your heart can constrict, and you grow bitter, or there can be an expansion and a life lived fully. You are not ever, were not ever, a composite of others' opinions: you are and *were you*. So yes: go forward in rage and create things and make it better for others.

I return to the dream of my years.

The dream goes like this: I am in a field. The kind of field varies. It is beautiful. Then I realise I am very young and I am

97

not alone there, by choice: I have been left. I feel sensations of warmth, and then the cold comes, because I call out, and three pairs of eyes look at me in frigid disgust. They shame me. I have a sense of things beyond the field and people, but I cannot connect with them or touch them. The eyes look again, and then they turn to one another and are warm and smiling. There is laughter, but the laughter is mocking. I tend to wake up then; you can ask my husband, and he will tell you that I am crying. He has been settling me for twenty years. I try to prepare myself for this dream by imagining a different sort of field or insisting that it happen in my sea cave, where movement is only single file, so no one is admitted; I am enclosed but among friends, and it is too narrow to look around and see the faces; too noisy with the rush of the waves and the seabird colonies overhead to hear the mocking laughter.

But you cannot tell dreams what to do: it does not work like that!

I think that the fear accounts in part for the way I have always wanted to incorporate myself into the natural world. Touching, scratching, collecting, reading, sniffing and, especially in the case of seaweeds on the beaches, particularly my most-loved Pembrokeshire beaches and estuarine places, biting. Sucking. It transported me and simultaneously brought me back to myself.

There is a part of the world, on the upper Cleddau estuary, that I have always loved. Before I was born, my grandmother and great-grandmother lived here. It is a place of dense woods and rich, luxurious mud. At the quay, at this place, I had always felt something profound was happening, something wild and brilliant. That the curlews screamed and harangued the foolish people that came that way; that moss and weed grew fast and that the kelp was thrown up too far and too thickly;

the pink thrift too vigorous. There were things that were alive – or more than alive; a preternatural world, but whether wholly good or bad, I could not, as yet, translate. And the things that were long dead walked with as much colour and vehemence as the present living. I thought I felt a hunger in the land around me. As you see, I was a child of somewhat wild imagination.

Around here – and forgive me; you may find this terribly stream of consciousness, but this is how my mind runs – I would think to myself, as the salt slapped me, the trees suck air, and, at night, when the last shriek of the plump and pretty-breasted curlew is drawn from its throat, and when the strand-line treasure is dulled and shredded against the rock, even in fair weather, well then. When the moss spawns bad, it creeps across your foot if you slowly move, so be sure to move quite fast. When the twilight stalks, then that is the time. When the jewel sky and the lapping wing have beat their very blood into the hour, take heed. There is a wild rebellion here.

I would say all this, mouthing it. I expect this sounds odd or unbelievable to many readers, but this was how it was. When I learned languages in school, I would try to translate thoughts about landscapes like this and mouth those too. I did it through my teens, and I have never told a soul that is what I did, until now, on this page.

And I was scared, then. But I was not *only* scared. I was thrilled. I still hunger for rough weather and kelp to chew on and suck. I adore the slap of water weed on my legs in a stream or river, and I adore it in the sea, where it grows thick and wild. If I walk in a wood and see a mound of violets, I will hunger to bury my face in them and inhabit them. If their scent is invigorated by warmth, it is intoxicating. My fear, my bad fear, in these places, was all connected with my parents, not with the beautiful sea and salt world. (Although, of course, it is more complicated than that.) On the worst days, with the coldest of eyes and curses, curses, curses, I would walk on the coast path, and the Irish sea taunted me, and the kelp threatened to drown me, and I would look at the deep pools on the beach and think about drowning myself in them. But then I would think about the strange unspoken hangings, shootings, misplacings and agrestal illness in tidy family fields, and think *no*: poor things.

Also, if I brought to bear hard thought and ran down to the beaches and chewed on some harvest of the sea, I felt bonded to the place and, thus, comforted. You have to cook many of them, but I would pull a little laver off the rocks and suck on it, or gutweed, but it was the hefty chewy plants I loved best: oarweed, kelp and the types of wrack, or the red dulse. A chef or forager might tell you that it is not actually the salt that makes these so delicious and arresting, but the glutamates, but it is the salt and the sea I tasted and the promise these things held – of deep sea and wild places and of things that are good at surviving.

Before Christmas last year, I had just a few days on my own on the beaches of South Pembrokeshire. I arrived exhausted, but within a day or two, my colour was different. There were high winds at night and, in Broad Haven North, below the mediaeval church of All Saints Church at Walton West wherein lie or are commemorated, my grandmother and great-grandmother, cousins, aunts and uncles, great aunts and uncles: I walked out early in those winds to feel the salt slap. Not a soul about. In the night, the slap again as pieces of kelp and wrack flew across the road and onto the building, and in the morning, the road was decorated with small pebbles and, in places, big seaweed branches. I had laver bread with bacon and eggs, and out I went. To walk some sections of St Bride's Bay. Again, not a soul about. It was glorious. These places are full of difficult memories and sensation – as I said above, it is complicated – but they are exquisite, and I fight to distinguish the two. Sharing them all with my children and husband has helped me towards new and fresh ways of seeing them, too, and I am thankful for that.

Oh, what the natural world gifts you. It looks after you if you will only be sensible enough not to look after it back. I do not mean that it is benevolent because that suggests something about our even being worthy of that and, frankly, I see nature as bigger than us, and we have only been here in a glimmer of its developing time, as we grow more stupid, wreaking havoc upon it; a havoc which I cannot forgive. And yet and yet: here in these wild places, there is bounty and deep peace. There is 'God or whatever means the good' in a line from a favourite MacNeice poem,[32] where time can stop, the heart can understand and the body is at peace. Do read it and do so aloud.

For years, I have heard the rhythm, the iambic tetrameter of this poem, and felt it hard. I adore the idea of time and context stopping for love and the body being at peace. Now, in December high winds, alone and out in the salt, I hear it again. I think I am all about cold days and strandlines and walking against the window; jubilant nature and books, always books, held against my heart and thought like a talisman, sometimes. Lines from books, from texts, are like that for me, springing up. Pushing hard against the cold, there is a peace of the body, also, which settles a restless mind. If I looked out across the beach at St Bride's, I would see a low expanse of rocks, and

32. 'Meeting Point', verse seven from *Louis MacNeice, Collected Poems*, Faber & Faber, repr. 2002.

I remember being very frightened because I was thrown off those rocks to make me learn to swim. I had plimsolls on, and I remember them swelling with water, my clothes ballooning out. The water was shallow, but I did not know that; I only knew that I was scared. I tried to say but was laughed at; they must have known I was not in danger, but I did not. Someone who was there hauled me out and told me I was pathetic. The same person with whom I had been, though very little, on nearby beaches. Once, a young child in the family was cheeky, with perfectly normal, spirited child cheek, and the same person picked up the child and threw him into a freshwater stream cutting swathes into the sand. The child was fully clothed and wearing an overcoat because, though it was summer, the weather was appalling. I remember being very shocked and the child grinning somehow and telling no one. But twenty-five years later, that child remembered it, and we talked about it. And I wanted to talk more about the not-telling, but you see, there is a lot of life to live, and you cannot always bring your grief, your confusion, and your rage to the surface: these things will come, often enough, unsummoned.

I looked at the rock I had been chucked off again now. I thought I had the right rock. It was just a rock. One of the things about depression is that you cannot just look at a thing and the thing be in its own self: the ghosts come by for you, and there is this painful nostalgia of, say, this rock or this tree, and back come the pounding feelings. But it is not fair and, anyway, a beach, rock, tree – a place – is broader than that, so you have that horrid recollection, do a sharp intake of breath, and on you go, moving fast maybe, in the body's peace and safety; chewing on your wrack or kelp, if you like and happy in the salt slaps to your face. There is grace, but it does not come to you, I have found. You must go and find it, in a place or in your imagination which is a storehouse for all your life.

Stars. Finding routes home, tilting your head for the Plough and comfort in Sirius: scale and light in trying to find joy in darkness

Nature is made to conspire with
spirit to emancipate us.

There is a children's book which I continued to read long after I was too old to read it. I might look again tonight, as today has not been the best of days, and I have been quaking in my boots. A series of stimuli again and a bad night. One thing to remember is that, as I write this book, *These Envoys of Beauty*, I am looking back, but I am also in a present where I am not wholly well. Moreover, in that present, I have three sons, and one of them was very unwell for three years and is still recovering. And I am a SEND parent. There are days when I am on my knees; the additional caring made hard by the decade it has taken to find answers, the legwork, passionate defence and defiance I had to have in the face of a lot of naysayers. We will return to this. Back to the owl and dark and stars – because it was from this book that I first learned about constellations and went on to watch them as closely as I could, wherever I was in the world and to make a note of meteor shower dates –

which is how I came to be on the Preseli mountains or a beach in Pembrokeshire at night in mid-August.

The children's book I mentioned is called *The Owl Who Was Afraid of the Dark*[33] and is about an owl called Plop whose wise mother instructs him to pop off and find out about good things. It is pretty, instructive and, at one point, truly melancholy. 'I don't want to be a night bird,' Plop told his mummy. He finds dark nasty but is counselled by his mother that this is an assumption and to test it out. She tells him he had better find out about the dark before he makes up his mind. The little owl finds out marvellous things about the dark from a small boy who is looking forward to campfires and fireworks, from an old lady – this is the bit I find melancholy – who says that she loves the dark because DARK IS KIND. She can dream and forget that she is old and, instead, sit and remember all the good times. And as I write this, I suppose this does say dreadfully melancholy things about being older – which Dorothy Rowe, whom you have already met, had reassured us in *Depression: The Way out of Your Prison*, that ageing came with benefits and good things too) and from a young girl who emphasises the necessity of dark because otherwise Father Christmas cannot come and fill your stocking. But it was the last visit that I found most compelling. Partly because it was about the luminous and extraordinary shapes and designs of our world and because it was an adult with a hobby. Nice adults with hobbies were really important to me as a child and young person because, I think, I was born old and did not always understand or feel at all understood by other children, and partly because, although it took a long time before I could identify the nub of the problem (I might have been born old,

---

33. *The Owl Who Was Afraid of the Dark*, Jill Tomlinson, Puffin, 1973.

but I was still not particularly experienced or clever), adults who connected with me warmly were in short supply.

So, I particularly liked the kind and responsive astronomer who talked to the little owl: To 'What's that you've got there?' He patiently explains that he has a telescope and that it is for looking at the stars and planets at night. Then, in response to the nervous little owl telling him that he does not like the dark, the man promises him that DARK IS WONDERFUL, and he shows Plop lots of stars and how they made patterns in the sky, pointing out the bright Pole Star, the Plough, the Dog Star and Orion the Great Hunter.

I remember where I was. In bed, feeling nervous as I often did and afraid of the dark, but more afraid of the world day *or* night, because one thing my mother did when I was told off was to escalate things quickly so that behaving badly would be about being a bad child, would be about being born a bad child, a wicked child and, what is more, that it was visible to everyone. While my mother hit me and kicked me, pinched me hard and pulled at my hair, it was this spite which felled me and which I am breathing through carefully as I write these words for you. You see, I felt unsafe, that no one could genuinely love me or accept me, whether adult or child, and that made my place in the world insecure. Still, my parents were not without kindness, and I had lovely books – such as this one. But they are always going to be a bit tainted, aren't they? You feel they did you a kindness not because you deserved it but because they were good people who had been cursed by you. It's terribly dramatic, but that's what was in my head. This lovely book about the owl gave me the skies. A whole new world and, because it was so expansive, a liberation and that thing I have mentioned before in this book: the comfort of scale. That I was tiny and inconsequential meant the other things, including all the bad things and the hurts, and the people were inconsequential too. This was an encouraging thought.

I lived very rurally, so I had a good view of the stars. I would identify Venus, the evening star, then look for the pole star, understanding its importance for navigation for millennia and imagining the history of tall ships and lemons to protect against scurvy and ships' cats (remember I was very young at the time). Orion, if you look at him, is big and stately and busy. He is off for the night and not afraid of the dark, or anything for that matter. His belt points to Sirius, the dog star, whom I felt was his hunting dog and loyal companion. I would tell myself these stories, only later learning that Sirius, who is also called Alpha Canis Majoris or the Dog Star, is the brightest star in the night sky, with an apparent visual magnitude of –1.46. It is a binary star in the constellation Canis Major. The bright component of the binary is a blue-white star twenty-five. Four times as luminous as our Sun. I will go out and see him tonight, I think. I learned that Orion was located on the celestial equator – I so enjoyed the notion that both the globe and the sky had an equator (and celestial equator is the most arresting phrase, isn't it?) – and visible throughout the world. Wherever I was in the world, I could look at him and know that his brightest stars are blue-white Rigel and red Betelgeuse. As for the plough or the Big Dipper, I just thought it looked friendly and playful and waited and understood that it was a pattern within a greater constellation of Ursa Major, the Great Bear. Still, I use it to find my way to other stars in exactly the way I did as a child.

There is deep wonder when you understand, or begin to understand, that the light you see is ancient. That it emanated when velociraptors roamed about, when where I live was under sea. Looking *up* and so *back* is thrilling because these are the most ancient things I see. Because you may be looking at this piquant luminosity, yet it may emanate from something which is no longer there, from a star which died a long time ago or is transmuted into a different form from when it emitted that light, and the process goes on even though we are not there to witness it. Moreover, I have always found solace in the wonder of the empty spaces between stars, or rather, wonderfully full spaces whose contents are not yet fully accounted for and never will be. We know that historically and in diverse cultures now, the shapes and spaces between stars are also their own shapes: this different, this beautiful other of interpretation grips me.

When I first saw Carl Sagan present his *Cosmos* on television[34] and watched his warm and loving descriptions of the known universe, I sat there open-mouthed. He was an expert, yet it was as if he were seeing it for the first time: he was knee-deep in the love of it. He said, 'We are related in the most intimate way'. And, 'We are all of us solar-powered'. And he said, of the stars, 'We are their children'. 'We are made of star stuff', and the penny dropped. I saw patterns and ancient things; I gradually understood that the stars in patterns or constellations were not cosied up near (relatively!) to one another but light years away from one another, only looking like a pattern to us; I understood that what we are made of was forged in the

---

34. *Cosmos: A Personal Voyage*, by Carl Sagan, Ann Druyan, and Steven Soter, with Sagan as presenter. PBS, 1980. I also watched Kenneth Clark's Civilisation, Jacob Bronowski's *The Ascent of Man*, and David Attenborough's *Life on Earth*, but Cosmos blew them out of the water, and I still wanted Sagan to be my dad because then we could have gone on astrophysics day trips and he seemed extraordinarily gentle and kindly and wore his scholarship lightly while wearing questionable anoraks.

hearts of stars and, finally, as I watched Sagan tilt his face to the sun, or gentle handle a blade of grass as he sat on a clifftop, quoting Walt Whitman (whom I also came to love fifteen years later), I desperately wished that Carl Sagan had been my dad or at least a kindly uncle.

Stars. Sometimes I cried at night. We had a patio outside our house at the top of a steep valley, and I would sneak out and look at the stars as I did that crying. When I was at university, I discovered Dante, and it was the sections about stars, being guided to them, which brought me up short. Let me share these passages with you now:[35] The first is the verses end of Inferno, from *The Divine Comedy* and the second the last cantos of Paradiso:

> *There is a secret for you to discover:*
> *'My guide and I started out on that road,*
> *Through its obscurity to return to the bright world;*
> *And not worrying about taking any rest,*
>
> *We mounted up, he first and I second,*
> *So that I saw some of the lovely things*
> *That are in the heavens, through a round opening;*
>
> *And then we emerged to see the stars again.*
> *At this point high imagination failed;*
> *But already my desire and my will*
> *Were being turned like a wheel, all at one speed,*
>
> *By the love which moves the sun and the other stars.*

---

35. My copy is Dante *The Divine Comedy*, translated by C.H. Sisson, Pan Books, 1981.

This is not a scholarly comment, more something which is about emotional impact. Those cantos made me think of a journey, a secret, and a knowing, numinous and animated by love. I have always struggled with faith – and believe me, I have tried – but on my worst days, as a child, young person, adult, mother, in despair or when I could not corral the movements of a hectic mind, the notion that there was a prime mover behind natural forms and there, turning the stars, went some way to set me straight. It prompted me to feel a little better, less alone, and then experience the animus to find that love, in rosebay willowherb or Sirius, as I imagined him scampering in his dwelling, as all creatures do. A great constellation in the sky with its friendly hound, countless light years away,[36] but near and confidential, in my thoughts.

I, too, scamper in my dwelling, sometimes safe, sometimes not, but at least with the knowledge of how to reach quietly for some succour: out there and *up* there.

And in *here*, because didn't Sagan explain how we are made of 'star stuff'?

---

36. Sirius is 8.6 light years from Earth, meaning that if you were travelling at around 40,000 mph, it would take 296,000 years to reach the little fellow. Apologies: I did not even have to look this up, and I hope that fact will have sent a thrill along the spine of nerds everywhere.

(Home: 'Bookworm Towers'. I am burying it in green.)

A Conclusion

Nature, in its ministry to man, is not only the material but is also the process and the result.

Let me end by tying together all the themes in these stories and an explanation of the joy and sustenance of reading nature, being in it and seeing its (impersonal) prompts to a better life. To do so, I will take you into some unpromising places and show you some sad things. Also, to do so, I think it might help to revisit the idea – in Dorothy Rowe, *Depression: The Way out of your Prison* – that our understanding of our world is predicated on what we have seen, experienced and understood.[37]

It took me decades even to think that just because I felt something that did not mean the feeling was based on something real and true and the very idea was liberating; that I could try to unmake things, deconstruct things, just as I had constructed them using the best materials I had. When I was supported well by a psychotherapist, for the first time after a breakdown when the youngest of my three was seven months

---

37. Dorothy Rowe, Ibid., p.15. '...if you believe that the world *is* the way you see it then when the world changes you feel frightened and lost.'

old, and by a clinical psychologist much later, we discussed this. We talked about identifying patterns, images, traps: we went back, into the present, and then we tried to make a new future. I am not there, and I think, as I have said earlier in this book, that we have more work to do on those ghastly flashbacks I still get. Nonetheless, I am on the way and with the help of the fine things around me. From my reading,[38] if I have it right, the brain creates a believable experience. As we navigate the world, we may assume that we are experiencing it exactly as it is, but our sensory information is incomplete, and we are only seeing glimpses of physical reality. Now, the brain does intelligent things and fills in the blanks, and so, in fact, our world is predicated on what our brain guesses or anticipates or what it adds to with layers of empirical experience unique to us as an individual.

It is fascinating, if terrifying, to understand this concept and, also, to try to see the world differently – and even then, know that you will only have partial glimpses.

Ah, but your glimpses could be *so much better*.

Let me elaborate.

I had a visit to psychiatric outpatients at the local hospital and felt a quickening, a lightening, as I came out. It was a new world pulsing away; a rebellious idea that I could have been wrong in constructing my world, knowingly or not, around the idea of myself as a loathsome creature; a bringer of harm. The press of that on your heart and head and the way it stops you from trusting in or bonding with others is horrible, though I always, *always* tried. When I look back, and even now if I am not careful, I feel a tremendous need to atone for all the wrong

---

38. I recommend Christian Jarrett's *Great Myths of the Brain* (Wiley-Blackwell, 2014). Jarrett is a cognitive neuroscientist, editor and author who writes with beguiling clarity and warmth.

things I did and *was*: I thought I had done more bad things than anyone else I knew. And sometimes, the atonement has been exhausting because I have taken on the care of too many and too much and made myself ill in the process. Here I was, letting go a bit, but scared of embracing a bold and different world. What does this part of the story have to do with the natural world?

Well now. It is and was, for me, about feeling and properly looking, sometimes in unpromising places – because it is all very well my talking about lovely places and thinking about lovely places and suggesting you go there on a wing in your imagination, but we must work with what we have, too. Otherwise, what am I saying to everyone about privilege and physical freedom? We do not all have that.

On one particular day, and when I was very unwell, I had a dismal garden outside the psychiatric wing of a large hospital.

It was a depressing, scrubby garden. I called it, on my visits to the doctor here, The Viburnum Jungle. Just as my father had loathed lilies, I have always thought viburnum – I believe this one was a *Viburnum × burkwoodii* – a loathsome plant. It is a pointless municipal parks and gardens plant; its leaves invite you to take no joy in their texture; its flowers are assertive but never pretty – it is a means to an end: a plant of no beauty. It was here in abundance before the psychiatric wing, and, worse, it was smothering some rock roses planted near it, swooping down and killing them with shade and ugliness. Shiny emerald leaves, curling brown at the edges; clouds of white flowers with a dull sepia tone to their edges. Below the viburnums, with the dying rock roses, were the yellowed leaves of daffodils that must have flowered once but gave up, gasping, sandy soil, cigarette butts and a Twix wrapper. It seemed to go with the decoration in psychiatric outpatients, too; there were little glass vases of single artificial flowers in that strange clear substance which pretended to be water. A gel. I had seen much of this fake solid-water stuff in various municipal rooms with flip charts. So that is what I had, and I thought about what was in front of me and tried to see it in a new way and embellish it with new thought. Tried to say to myself, *Have you been seeing this place right?* No, not the rubbish and the B&H packets and a bit of vape detritus and Chupa Chups sticks, but soil and roots, variegation on leaves and the determination of the plant to push up. I thought about the roots of trees and shrubs entwining and passing by and making room, and I thought about the emerald in the leaves, which led me to gemstones and things that sparkled and deep water and fantastical, glorious, imagined things. Is this twee? This is how it was because this is what was there, and this was where it led.

I think of explorations from Richard Mabey's *Nature Cure*[39] that when healing came, it was not a sense of being taken not out of oneself, but, instead of going back in: nature enters us if we allow it and fires up the wild bits of our imagination: this is how it has always been for me, though I cannot say I am healed because there are things which still need attention. I think of it as an ongoing process and, in the worst times, as a child, a young person, now, as things held at bay because of the worlds I choose to inhabit and which fire up my imagination, as well as comfort and distract me. It is a multisensory experience, as I hope I have shown, a beautiful and necessary thing.

There's something else, from one of the finest books on personal experience of depression that I know, *Sunbathing in*

---

39. Ibid., p.218.

the Rain: A Cheerful Book about Depression by the Welsh poet Gwynneth Lewis.[40] Something particularly helpful in this book, in its clear message as it begins, is the prompt to see the value in how you are feeling and reacting in depression. That is, you are warmly encouraged to see what you are being taught. If you can cope with the internal winter of depression, then depression can be a friend. This is not to say that we welcome depression or wish it on anyone, but that if it should descend, we watch and listen and come to understand that the way in which we have been living is unbearable, something not for us. Thus, depression may teach you how to live in a way that suits you so much better. The point is also that if you do not listen, it comes back again and again until the point is received and acted upon.[41]

I think this is right and enormously comforting. That you have to listen, and you need to see, and I suppose that's what I've been saying all the way through this memoir. The natural world around me has been my guide, and it has sustained me. In it, wherever I was, I was better able to use the prompts of my mind to make and remake new things and find ways that *were* for me. That involves reflection and honest contemplation of the self. You might like the people around you, the fam-

---

40. *Sunbathing in the Rain: A Cheerful Book about Depression*, Harper Collins, 2002, p.xiii – as quoted in Dorothy Rowe – Ibid. – who hugely admired this book.

41. It is important for me to say something about antidepressant medication here. Or rather, to say nothing other than explain myself in this context. I have never taken a medication which has helped me, other than for its sedative purposes at bedtime. Trazodone, if you are interested. *You* may have found a successful regimen, though we know we still must do the work of unpicking what is wrong: we do what works for *us*. I take a low dose of amitriptyline at night to settle the worst antics of hypervigilance, which is worse at that time. I do not take it at antidepressant level but to sedate.

ily, the family friends who were there when it all began, to start seeing or at least to consider that they might have misunderstood what was going on in your world when you were little, when it all began, and as you grew, but this is not a reasonable expectation.

Often, even to be understood is not a reasonable expectation. *People will say, I did not see that, you have it wrong, you misremembered* or, *if that had happened, I would have known.* They do not mean to gaslight you, but to reflect on the fact that they ought to have protected you in certain ways is painful; moreover, it may be troubling and destabilising for another person to rethink someone they felt they knew well and loved deeply. Surely that beloved person or those beloved people could not do something like that? If they could do that, what else? *Too terrible to think about!* Thoughts are shut down. I understand it, and I do not want other people to be hurt. Nonetheless, it smarts not to be able to tell a story or to have to listen repeatedly to stories which are not true. So, I have had to think about how I would master myself and try to think clearly and use what I was feeling. I am sure I was frequently depressed as a child and adolescent and had periods of depression in adulthood, too, though not for some time when I have instead been sad because of circumstance, and that is *different.* But you have *you* and many wonderful things about you, and to know that just as you created views and ideas about yourself and the world, so, as I have said, via Dorothy Rowe, you are free to change them. Depression can end. Much, otherwise, can be lived with. A life with limits is still a rich life.

Find a way to tell your story, and even if there is bad faith or misunderstanding in your family or in your immediate context, whatever that may be, you are not without voice. What has this to do with the natural world? Observation of it all, close watching of its brilliant phenomena, and gauging of pattern and order have given me courage. Moreover, beauty sustains you and gives you some vigour and solidity. I do believe that, though I know that sometimes we must look for that beauty in unpromising places. It is there. Remember the viburnum garden I wrote about earlier?

I wanted to end by sharing with you what I have felt compelled to build around us in our home and for our three boys, both as something nurturing and because it felt incumbent in environmental terms. It is about the natural world, and about what was healing for me, and what I regarded as resources for them. Also, it is telling a story – just not with words.

I was extremely unwell in my first pregnancy and after all three children, particularly after my third when, for a while, I failed to function altogether. I could not go very far from the house at those times because I felt unsafe. Then, the cutting, the scything, and the plague of 'letting in the light' – whereby anything which produced shade was removed – started happening all around me (I live in a terrace), where lawns were removed and filled with shingle, trees were radically lopped, the old walls full of wildlife taken down to be rebuilt and neatened. An ancient, gnarled lilac I had adored was gone, the Victorian apple tree which had been carefully espaliered years ago. Old windows went, too, in favour of newness and cleanness and used putty and paint and shored-up old mess. I am not saying this to evince any notion of superiority on my part but to show sadness and rebellion because I felt that, in neatening and calling to order, much was being damaged. It felt most painful during these periods of ill health. The scent of the old lilac had drifted across the surrounding gardens, too. It was that which made me particularly sad: there was no sense to its being hacked down, and a shared pleasure was surely gone.

It felt like vandalism, a desecration. There is nothing you can do and no rights that you have. I had to do something, however. And here it was. I was not the only one who felt sad.

On the front of our house was an old grapevine; planted, I often thought, by whoever it was that planted and espaliered the old apple trees here, of which only two remain. I grew the grapevine across the front of our house, over a frame and into the old apple tree which we had kept. There was pressure to take down the old apple tree, to let in more light, to neaten everything, and I made arguments for shade and dappled light; for wildlife and mini-beats and micro-organisms and said it was right for the children. Then, I grew a pear tree on the front of the house and espaliered that, and we admired its exquisite blossom. Together we planted densely and packed borders, harvested and swapped seeds and used wildflower mats and bombs. The boys and I threw seed in the borders and spent time looking at the big elder tree halfway down the garden. Elder, *Sambucus Nigra*, is underrated; perhaps because of its ubiquity and flimsy wood and, again, two of our neighbours had been saying it ought to come down to let in more light. But it *was* letting in the light.

Here is why.

Elder's soft wood houses many fungi and lichen; the tree has patches of all colours and is absolutely larded with bugs and small creatures. On the underside of its leaves, I would show the boys the ladybird larvae, larger than their parents and clinging on to the slightly viscous leaves. Sometimes we would bring some in to hatch in those little net pavilions you can buy, and my middle son was particularly fond of them, letting them fly from his bedroom window and, quite staggeringly, noting that in a crack in the plaster by his window, the ladybirds over-wintered – as if they come back to base to start it all again. The flowers provide nectar for a variety of insects, and the berries are eaten by birds and mammals. You should see the activity! Dormice eat both the berries and the flowers. Moth caterpillars feed on elder foliage, and the buff ermine is a pretty little thing, looking, I think, like a miniature Regency crinoline gown. But that is not all because our giant elder is also wonderfully, richly evergreen because I have grown the fast-scrambling evergreen clematis – *Clematis armandii* – up it. As a result, the top of the tree, which I can see from my writing desk, is a sort of patio to assorted birds and, most recently, a comical pigeon community. It brings me joy. When one of our neighbours was talking about why we should cut the tree down, they accidentally made it sound more attractive: *It is like a galleon, swaying in the wind sometimes.*

I love having the tree-galleon out there,I love seeing what comes up where and the faces of the celandines turned to the sun, the tiny plants that erupt between the old flags, and how lovely is dead nettle, with its purple and white flowers. How lovely are stinging nettles where I have left them because of the way in which they increase butterflies: Nettles are the food plant for the caterpillars of red admiral, small tortoiseshell, painted lady and comma butterflies, and we bolster that painted lady community by hatching additional larvae.

So, it is a tumble of plants and little ponds and big galleon trees and old things and nettles and thyme, marjoram, salvia, buddleia: things bees and butterflies will like. There is a resident hedgehog called Gavin (which is probably several different hedgehogs; varieties of Gavin, or 'Our Gav, the Hedgehog' as we say) and bats playing about and as much shade and mottled, dappled light as I can manage in a modest garden. It felt important to grow everything bigger and wilder when so much else was cut down, and now, in the summer, you enter through a green tunnel. It is a haven and a safe place and something we made. Sometimes, I was making it when not well, almost against my will, knowing deep inside me it was what we should do and what I needed.

Those Envoys of Beauty.

Why did I choose this as my title? Here is the section from Emerson's *Nature* you might have seen in the epigraph:

> *To go into solitude, a man needs to retire as much from his chamber as from society. I am not solitary whilst I read and write, though nobody is with me. But if a man were alone, let him look at the stars. The rays that come from those heavenly worlds, will separate between him and what he touches. One might think the atmosphere was made transparent with this design, to give man, in the heavenly bodies, the perpetual presence of the sublime. Seen in the streets of cities, how great they are! If the stars should appear one night in a thousand years, how would men believe and adore; and preserve for many generations the remembrance of the city of God which had been shown! But every night come out these envoys of beauty and light the universe with their admonishing smile. (Ralph Waldo Emerson. From Nature, Chapter One.)*[42]

Now, Emerson asserts throughout *Nature* the primacy of spirit over matter. He posits that nature's purpose is as a representation of the divine, that it stimulates human insight into the

_____

42. Ibid., p.17.

laws of the universe and thus brings man closer to God. In this, Emerson is expressing the philosophy of transcendentalism, having gradually moved away from the religious and social beliefs of his contemporaries. He came to believe that the Divine suffuses nature, in the divinity of nature. That is not all that transcendentalism is, and its exploration would be one for another book, but this element is that which is relevant to this memoir. I find it thrilling and comforting. That we are surrounded, and nature is a broad church and excludes no one. There is something in Nature – as he moves through its sections (Commodity, Beauty, Language, Discipline, Idealism, Spirit, Prospects) that is so hopeful; so energetic and joyous, and he begins his conclusion with, 'The aspect of Nature is devout...'[43] and it is something we all share.

I have always felt a generosity around me, and that I was less lonely outside; at the very least, I could find something to comfort me – like the time I sucked on the gorse flowers when feeling desperately alone with a father. Illness, disability, chronic illness, caring for someone whose world has turned upside down so young – all those things make you solitary and separate you in a crowd. I from you; the other. Which are you? Are you the other, or is it me? The sense that you must work closely with your imagination made me solitary for a long time, and, while not infrequently lonely, I have banked up resources through necessity and could be happily alone, solitary, for days – weeks even. If I looked up, what would I see? We are too often desensitised to the beauty of this world. Because we are selfish and self-absorbed but also because its beauty is so prolific, broad, and mysterious: we are immured to it. If the stars were an occasional spectacle, we would mar-

43. Ibid., p.47.

vel, but we fail to do so because of their ubiquity. He does not speak directly of faith, but there is a generous and hopeful sense of collective consciousness here if we would stand close to extraordinary things. For me, having been bothered and repeatedly felled by mental health problems, it is enormously hopeful, even in the face of the devastation we have wrought and which we understand now. Yes, even in the face of that. And all my life, survival, self-reliance, and recovery have been rooted in the natural world.

'The stars awaken a certain reverence, because though always present, they are inaccessible; but all natural objects make a kindred impression when the mind is open to their influence.'[44]

Nature has not cured me, as I have been keen to emphasise. Still, as I write now, I am looking at the early spring garden and the growing, budding green mass of our own modest garden, and I am intensely grateful for what has been about me all my life; midges above the river Frome as light fades, razor clams bubbling up on the Pembrokeshire coast. My sea caves, mud, flood, and weeds. Igniting my imagination and keeping me safe for just a little while longer. I will always do what I can to return the favour.

And you know, lately, I have been wondering if I am wrong about viburnum. That I ought to appreciate it more. Even in the most unpromising place, nature inches in, and there are things to look at and cherish in the least beautiful natural forms if we would only look.

This book is about being observant. About looking carefully and being on guard, because the workings of nature are also surreptitious. Is nature a cure? For some, but not for me,

---

44. Ibid., p.17.

as I have said earlier. Permit me, if you will, to end with some short related sections from my own novel, *Saving Lucia*,[45] which explores, partly, what it is to be mentally unwell, to be assumed thus, who gets to decide (in which way it is a historical survey) and the notion of being broken, or breaking, but nonetheless being out in the world and doing what you can, however small. Trying to work, write, teach, keep friends – the latter has surely not been possible – and raise a family in which there are additional needs.

'...she was effective in her work although she was never wholly well, not always, yet I was ill, again and again. I did not, as these doctors might have thought, get fully well. Yet I did not give up: I had purpose, and there was work, so much work, to be done. Well enough and full of purpose.'

'I have learned, and I won't have been the only one, that you do not have to be completely well to care, love, or dance. To work. And anyway: define well. Then mad. I challenge you.'

If you are finding days difficult as you read this, know that I do too – but go out and have confidence in that ragged, broken self.

Will you join me to look at the stars, these envoys of beauty, on a clear night?

---

45. *Saving Lucia*, Bluemoose Books, 2020. I keep signed copies in my favourite bookshop for you: https://mrbsemporium.com/

Epilogue

I hope, dear reader, you have enjoyed this short book and that you take from it only comfort. Because of its context, of sad things, of which I have only skated on the surface, I have barely touched on questions of climate change and its impact on places I record or species I watch and love. Instead, I have tried to record faithfully what we are making around us here and what I have tried to make around my children, the main stimulus for which was environmental and the work on which is ongoing. I thought, also, that I would suggest things for good days and bad days. I am not a counsellor or health professional, but I am recording things I do now as part of learned experience; that is, small practices which calm me down and settle me: this is all part of my memoir and what I hoped it might record. Just four things, and all very much focused on my senses.

One. On a flower. I particularly love this with a peony, but you could pick any flower which appeals to you. It works best when that flower has layers of petals in the way a peony does. My favourite is the dark *Red Charm*, with its luscious bowl of large, deep red petals filled with deep red staminodes.[46]

---

46. *Paeonia lactiflora* 'Red Charm'.

Two. A riverbed and bring a child if you have one or can borrow. Get into a stream, any stream. Feel it, dam it, bathe in it: do whatever you feel. Make it cold if you can and go to its edge, lounging against its banks. and, however much the sadness has been claiming you, you will, I promise, find comfort. It's good to regress, too. Overall, children are better than adults, I have found, and they remind you that paddling is one of life's greatest pleasures.

Three. Moss and lichen. Find a wall, for richness of texture, an old wall and look at it as you have never done before. Feel the moss and creep up on it, pressing it down, and if you do this gently enough, you feel it bounce back like it is answering or rebuffing you for being so bold. Now touch the lichen, feeling its flakes and whorls and do it slowly. Truly, when I really do not know what to do – and I've done it tonight because my son is struggling so much (there is much to tell about my family, but I have not done so because of agency) – here is something I do. Will you try it? The contrast is great, but I would not want you to have anxiety about finding both.

Four. Rock strata on a cliff. I have found that observation of order and layers, because I cannot get away entirely from difficult mental health, has made me a keen amateur geologist. That and an appreciation of scale because seeing how tiny I am and we are. If you went to Charmouth in Dorset, for example, then the rocks in the cliffs and on the beach at Charmouth are the remains of an ancient Jurassic Sea; you would be looking at many layers of sediment laid down in an ocean around 195 million years ago. They contain lots of fossils, and for years I have been finding them on the beach. The tall cliffs at Monknash, that is Cym Nash, on the Glamorgan Heritage coast between Cardiff and Swansea, are limestone formed in the Carboniferous Period (350 million years ago) and Blue

Lias of the Liassic period (180 million years ago). You can read those cliffs in fantastic stripes, and just standing there, observing, is soothing and grounding. Stories still and settle you, don't they?

I suppose that this is what I am trying to say.

Observing. Reading.

Just seeing, wherever you are. Being in it, wherever you are. Those things are the finest of company.

Favourite places

I thought I would describe these – just places in the British Isles – that I know well for the purposes of telling you about them and how much I love them. They are the places in the book. I do want to say something about this, however, as I know I am lucky, and while I must pace and be careful, I can go. I understand not everyone can travel, and many are not well enough to leave the house. When I was writing *These Envoys of Beauty*, I asked others if I should try to write about these places differently in terms of suggesting diverse ways of visiting them – including in imagining them. I asked writer friends who are disabled and chronically ill; those who are largely or mostly bedbound. *Write about your experience and use your voice as the answer. Do not try to write for anyone else.* So here we are. I wanted you to know I had been thinking about it all.

I thought about many places which I hold close to my heart and, indeed, you have met several of them through the book, but here are some specifics in case you would like to visit them. They are listed because they are places I have visited many times, so I realise the geographical variation is not great. Part of the reason for this is that, unexpectedly, I have come to roost and raise our family near to where I was born, so I have shared things with my boys and been helped to see them in a new light, through their eyes. Or, more accurately, partly so. But still, I have been able to add their responses to the pictures in my head and store them up; things to draw on, you might say. A shifted and multivarious scrapbook.

I have given simple map numbers for each place; in case you would like to walk and explore. I would like to think of you exploring these few places because, in that way, you are walking through the book.

Iford. Wiltshire

The River Frome at Iford. Here is a place, on the river Frome, where my lifetime friend of a river flows fast. There is a particular place where you climb down by a lane, and the nettles are thick, the mud likewise at the edge of the river. When I was a child, I used to imagine that characters from The Wind in the Willows lived around this area. I was sure it was set on the Wiltshire-Somerset border. Visiting this area again in lockdown with my youngest son, I felt a memory, a shiver of that. Was there a rat sculling out with a picnic basket? I read my favourite passages from the book repeatedly as a child for comfort. I have a theory that books – and especially their most loved section – are like talismans for a frightened child. For me, the more secluded episodes were the most comforting because I also longed for small, secluded spaces; often, I linked those spaces with childhood reading, and those early links resonate still.

If you want to visit this area and see what I saw and see, climb down into the river and wade left until it is too deep and fast or right to the bridge and, in hot summers, until you are in sight of the weird beyond. There are kingfishers here and, in the meadows around, a rich assortment of butterflies.

(OS Map 156: Chippenham and Bradford on Avon.)

Bookworm Towers. Or more to the point, its greenery. Wiltshire

Our house. Once upon a time, I bought a mid-eighteenth-century semi-derelict pub. Or rather, I bought two-thirds of it, as it had, at some point in its life, been converted into two cottages. Then, as I tended its wild garden and as I described earlier in this book, everyone cut the trees down and pushed down old Victorian garden walls to have them rebuilt tidily so there were straight lines where there had been none. There are days, still, when I am filled with fear, and it runs cold along my back and arms. Despite my years of work, I have never managed to rid myself of this. It is usually a cold look from someone, an item that reminds me sharply of my parents, usually my mother; sometimes words, but gestures will do. Three summers ago, we were in a beach house in America with my husband's extended family. Something about the atmosphere of that house that I could see my eldest – who went on to become seriously ill later that year – and a tension that could be acknowledged: the fear ran cold in me. A man came to the house to fix something and said it was not well built and that it would be knocked down. A combination of fear and disgust, I think, at the waste in an area of rough and colourful beauty on the Outer Banks of North Carolina, a finger of land into the sea, with the sea gradually reclaiming it all. I spent hours that night when the man had gone, shaking and crying; it all precipitated a series of panic attacks. Waste, coldness, flashbacks, cold eyes, trepidation about what I thought might happen with and for my son: too much.

Where am I going with this?

Whatever has happened in my life and continues to happen, in my raggedy home, I have shaken out seeds, reclaimed objects and made soft edges and hope for my sons, and it is my dear ambition, people who come here – such as those who attend community classes in our house too. The garden rushes in at the front door, unkempt but luscious. A gust of wind brings in tendrils from the grapevine this May as it makes its way along the front of the house and up towards the roof. Everything is blown big. These are soft things; I associate plants gone wild with generosity because of their sprawling and billowing nature. Also, plants pop up that you did not plant through self-seeding. Sometimes plants disappear altogether, but new ones come in their place. Like the redcurrant bush I did not plant, the foxgloves, and sunflowers. The natural world is so generous to us, though we are wasteful and often do not deserve it.

Now, if you are sad, lonely, and unwell while reading this, may I tell you something? That there is a place for you in my house, and most of all, if you, like me, navigate fear, cold down your back and your arm. I see you.

Don't worry about the map; I will just invite you over. I will send Gavin the pigeon, who lives in the tallest tree: he has potential as a carrier pigeon, and I can send him with a promissory note for tea and Welsh cakes plus directions because no one can ever find our house.

No map: it is hidden in plain sight, so I shall invite you. Shh now, though.

Barafundle Bay, Pembrokeshire

Here is another place of my heart, and there is something in the sweep of the headland and walk required to get to it which settles my heart. Up you go, past Stackpole Harbour, through a border of woods, up steep steps, and whoosh: onto an open headland. It is round and generous; you can see the rich strata in the cliffs about you and the red Pembrokeshire soil that I love so much. You walk over the undulating land, and then suddenly, there is a blot of azure just beyond you, and it reveals itself. There. Down you go, into that beautiful curve, hot white sand with caves at one end and clambering rocks at the other, above which the wood advances round the coast path. To me, a sense of relief, that heart settled. It is the curves, the open space, blue and red and the sharp pitch into that lovely curve of sand, where the bay water appears, as you round the headland above it, a preternaturally bright blue.

Oh my. It feels like freedom.

There is something else I relish here, which is the dunescape behind it. On paths through the dunes, you walk barefoot until the path becomes pricklier and pricklier on your feet; you are approaching a spar of the coast path and deep woods. Here with my youngest, on a warm spring day in 2022, we walked. We could smell the violets and the primroses before we saw the rush of bluebells. The woods were dark and cool, and we walked on, our feet getting filthier now, until we reached the first slope, then stopped, looking back at the ramsons, scenting those too; they – ransoms are wild garlic[47] – have been a joy all my life; they are pungent and pretty. Rebellion. I do not know if it's because of my past and the oddities of what's in my head, but I have always been cheered by this plant and others which spread and announce themselves so boldly.

---

47. Wild Garlic – Ramsons; *Allium ursinum* – are also known as Broad Leaved Garlic, Wood Garlic, and they flower between February and June. You can pick and eat every part of the plan – and I have done this ever since I was a child.

Will you go there? Or we could. I would like to talk more about the cliffs, the remains of an ancient beach, the choughs, and guillemots, and how they make me happy.

(OS Map 36 and Landranger 158.)

Newgale and my dream cave, St Brides Bay, Pembrokeshire.

I have referred in this book to my favourite sea cave at Newgale on St Bride's Bay in Pembrokeshire. I visit this beach as often as I can, at all tides, but especially when the tide is on the way out, and I can climb into and walk through the cave onto a beach which is not yet accessible by walking along the beach itself. Again, the constriction and cool darkness of that cave are richly rewarding, especially combined with the punch of the full beach beyond. It is the contrast: that is what I mean by the punch. It is contraction to expansion; to me, it feels like something on my pulse and a metaphor which is speaking to me.

You have been constrained; now out you go: you are safe.

It's born of being frequently ill and frequently feeling fearful and unsafe, which I would wish on no one and which I cannot expect anyone to understand. But beyond that narrow movement through the cave, you see something bright, for there is frequently a huge expanse of sand, smaller hidden places between rocks and a stretch of rockpools to explore, some of which are over your knees if you stand in them (I know this because I have fallen in them). I have never known eyes not to widen when I have shown others.

(OS Explorer Map 35.)

Patrishow Church, Black Mountains, Powys

Here is a place which I have salvaged from ruins and unkind words. I do not know if this means I found God, and that was the comfort – I mean, I hope this is what happened – but it is there, intact. There is a little lane after a drive through the Black Mountains of Powys, near to Abergavenny. At the bottom of that lane, there is a little stream, much overgrown – they are the best kind, I think – and with a wonderfully sandy, gritty bottom. As a child, I used to put my feet in that water and see how deep they would go; or I would feel the grit and sand on my hands. I have always wanted to feel texture, and even now, I cannot go onto a beach without rubbing a handful of its sand onto palms and wrists. I want to feel the natural world, to feel it, not just behold it.

By that lovely little stream, I remember times when my sweet-tempered lay preacher father laid it down to me, as my mother faced ahead, that I was here under sufferance, and they had not wanted me to be here. As a teenager, confused and lonely, I could not cry out at this, so I just dug my nails into my hands and made up my mind that if I ever had a child, I would not do this. Then, I comforted myself with the water, the sand, the grit – and the luxurious overgrowth around that water.

At the top of the lane is a church I would want you to see. The Church of St Issui, Partrishow, Powys, Wales, is a parish church dating from 1060. The existing building was mainly constructed in the fourteenth and fifteenth centuries and was restored in 1908–1909. The church is most famous for its rood screen, dating from 1500, but going through the lychgate and into the church, this was not what I wanted to see. I had a friend there and, yes, I know this is weird, but that is how I saw him. I was sure it was a *him*, and he said, *I am dead but see, I am still here*. The doom figure, dating from the seventeenth century, in sepia, a skeleton with defined ribcage, holding an hourglass and a knife. *That* was who I wanted to see.

Since I was very young, I have always wanted to see such creatures and to discover memento mori. This doom figure was painted on the liturgical wall at the rear of the church, so you saw him on the way out and in, but not during the sermon. These haunting wall paintings tell of the Last Judgement, and you can see them in a mediaeval church. This is the moment in Christian eschatology – the last things – when Christ judges souls to send them to either Heaven or Hell. But this memoir is about nature, and I am dwelling too long on interiors. Ah, it is all connected. Because the doom figure gave me urgency and whispered to me that things were passing, fleeting, and so was pain. So was loneliness. Then, I would go out into the churchyard, with the valley falling below me and knowing the favourite stream was there and the farmlands and mountains above me. I remember the sepia, the sand and grit and then the jonquils, because around Easter, it was exquisite. There were clouds of the tiny daffodils, and I would go searching for the best moss, looking for water and finding primrose banks and white and purple violets. It was, thus, a place of joy with doom at its heart. Go and explore and perhaps we can feel that contrast together, or know, as we walk, that fear and melancholy do not stop joy. Even depression has tiny windows, and they surprise us. I cannot escape hard memories, and I cannot escape the people or the stories that uphold falsehoods: that I was the bad child of good parents. What I can do is look at the sweep of the countryside around this gem of an old church with its doom figure telling you to reflect on your mortality and your forever and, if it is a warm day, we will be able to smell the slightly spicy scent of the primroses on the banks around the graves, and you will lie in the grass and on the moss bank and bury your face in a patch of violets and feel better, though our time is short.

It is because we know joy that we can illuminate pain. And because we know love, we know what love is not. And because life is fleeting, it is so fine, so precious. That life remains a blessing, although you cannot bless.[48]

(OS Explorer Map OL13: Brecon Beacons National Park/Parc Cenedlaethol Bannau Brycheiniog.)

Cresswell Quay. Pembrokeshire.

There is a reason why I made this the primary setting of my novel, *The Zebra and Lord Jones.*

Therefore, you and I need to go there. So, you give that novel a setting, and so you can see the place I will sketch below, an affair of the heart. Just a final place and that to which I am constantly returning to: my estuary. Again, it is in Pembrokeshire. I love the coast and have walked the coast path in its entirety, but there is another part of salt and mud which is life to me. It is hard to explain how deep it goes. Cresswell Quay is on one pill of The Daugleddau estuary. This estuary is the coming together of four rivers; the Western and Eastern Cleddau, Carew and Cresswell rivers, and while there's not a reach of it I do not like, its upper reaches of the Daugleddau estuary are particularly stunning; with steep, wooded banks alternating with gently sloping farmland. Most of the waterway is hidden away from the world: that is another reason I love it so. The quality of time stood still. Cresswell Quay, where the Creswell River pushes through the silt and mud, snaking around wooded banks, is where my grandmother lived for many years and my great-grandmother too. I did not know it when they lived there, but I knew it

---

48. A corruption of W.H. Auden's poem, 'As I Walked Out One Evening', from *Collected Poems of W.H. Auden*, Faber and Faber, 2007, should you wish to read the whole poem.

through her because she told me and told me and told. She was the greatest storyteller you ever did hear. If you go to this place, the woods rise on both banks, and at low tide, you cross the tributary stream across the steppingstones and move from one bank to another. The mud is ochre, it smells saline, and you hear the seabirds. Seaweeds are thrown up this high in stormy weather, and when the sun shines brightly on the low-tide mud, the tawny, russet, and ochre are silver-grey. It is quite a sight, and I anchor myself in that.

There is so much I do not understand about my family, but I feel a weight of history here, a dark, still beauty faintly, inchoately offering meaning to me in mud and wrack.

I have sometimes felt that home was inimical to my sense of home, so I recreated it in landscape: here is one place that I have claimed, and with the spirit of my grandmother and great-grandmother, I am not alone.

(OS Explorer Map: OL36: South Pembrokeshire.)

Resources

As this is a book about mental health, I wanted to offer you the resources I have found most useful when I was in need. Some of them are identified in the bibliography.

Samaritans. https://www.samaritans.org/ and 116 123. You do NOT have to be suicidal to call, and there are other ways to contact them that might suit you better and help you to process thoughts: you can write them a letter or email, and there is a particularly good app you can use.

Young Minds. If you are under twenty-five or perhaps the parent or carer of a child or young person with mental health problems or about whom you are concerned, there are huge resources here, plus a parent forum. https://www.young-minds.org.uk/

Family Lives. https://www.familylives.org.uk/ and 0808 800 2222. You can also email or use the live chat option. When my son is really struggling, and when I am, I rely on this organisation for reassurance, ideas, and comfort.

Mind. https://www.mind.org.uk/about-us/what-we-do/ People to talk to, advice and support, and importantly there is also a specialist legal line which provides information on mental health-related law to the public, service users, family members/carers, mental health professionals and mental health advocates. I found this extremely useful – and also saw how quickly we fall foul of it.

Shout on https://giveusashout.org/get-help/ and 85258 is, like the Samaritans, a twenty-four-hour service but is for text. It is a free, confidential, anonymous text support service. You can text from wherever you are in the UK, and it is for people in crisis.

With any of these, I have to say that if you think your life is at risk or think someone else's life is at risk, you must call 999, which is advice repeated across these services.

ACKNOWLEDGEMENTS

This book is for my husband Ned and my sons, Elijah, Isaac, and Caleb. I think a special thank you is due to the Recovery Team within our local mental health teams, and to those who have helped me along in primary and secondary mental health services and to advocate for me, including with GPs over the years. But particularly to the recovery service in Secondary Care, who worked with me with infinite care and compassion, humour and helped me to feel new and bed down some better ideas. While writing this book, my eldest was extremely un-well, and this was partly the prompt for the book: because he had been badly let down, I thought, by assorted agencies, and I wanted to turn fury and upset into positive things – which included *These Envoys of Beauty*, in many ways a paeon to beauty and a book about the observance of the structure and pattern – consoling when the world is chaotic and help is far away. For David Borrowdale at Reflex Press for taking on what was a new departure for his press and doing it boldly and lov-ingly. For my friends and my writing group. For them and for our community which has helped us look after one of our sons over a long period. Also, my many cousins and aunts and un-cles. I count those blessings often. To my brilliant agent Kate Johnson. While this was an independent project, she took a calm and loving interest in the book, as she does in all my work, and I am incredibly grateful. I love you all.